FIRMITAS UTILITAS VENUSTAS

ARCHITECTURE & SOCIETY

DAVID A. HANSER   CHERYL E. MORGAN

OKLAHOMA   STATE   UNIVERSITY

SCHOOL OF ARCHITECTURE

KENDALL/HUNT PUBLISHING COMPANY
Dubuque, Iowa

This edition has been printed directly from the authors' manuscript copy.

CONTENTS

PREFACE

We have developed this book to introduce architecture to the general public. We assume neither that the reader has any previous knowledge of the subject nor that the reader is a beginning architecture student. Technical aspects of architecture, such as construction and engineering, are presented as simply as possible and in only enough depth for the unitiated to understand what makes a building stay up and how the structure of a building can affect its appearance, how we react to it aesthetically.

Architecture is treated as a humanity in the broadest sense of the term. We use history as a framework to examine how architecture reflects the values of societies, past and present. We use historical examples to examine the variety of ways architects have housed us and our activities and given form to some of our aspirations and beliefs, but our book is not really an outline of architectural history -- if it were, it would be a much larger book.

If we do no more than help the reader enjoy the buildings he sees everyday and visits on his vacations, we feel we have accomplished a great goal, but we have two other, more pragmatic, goals. One is to give readers some idea of the services they may expect from an architect and enough of the special vocabulary he uses, both technical and formal, to be able to talk to him (and understand him). After all, many of the readers of this book will, as clients, directly confront architects. All readers have used and will continue to use architecture and, at least as taxpayers, pay for it. The more the reader knows about architecture, the better the building he can demand -- and get. In economic terms, this means more value for money spent. In spiritual terms, this means buildings which enrich ones life, which do more than just shelter activities.

Our second goal -- to "educate our future clients" -- may seem more selfish. It really isn't, since the result is better architecture for everyone. A client who is knowledgable about architecture is likely to choose an architect when he needs to build. A client who is familiar with what architects can do for him is likely to look for the best architect around -- rather than the first one listed in the Yellow Pages. And a client who enjoys architecture inspires the architect to do his best.

ACKNOWL- EDGMENTS

We would particularly like to thank Mark Robert Thompson who prepared the majority of the drawings for our book. Additional drawings were prepared by Timothy John Lovett, Wayne John Jacques, Dan Heidebrecht and William B. C. Harroff, who was also a great help in his other role as School librarian. John H. Bryant, Head of the School of Architecture at Oklahoma State University also deserves our gratitude for his forbearance as do other members of the faculty, especially James F. Knight, Alan W. Brunken and George W. Chamberlain, who read over parts of the manuscript. We thank them for their advice but do not hold them responsible for any errors. Richardson Rosecrans assisted us at a crucial point in the preparation of the manuscript.

INTRODUCTION

The buildings illustrated and discussed in this book were chosen because, in our opinion, they are especially clear and obvious examples of an architectural concept or because they help to explain the relationship between society and architecture particularly well. In most cases, they are also the most characteristic examples of a historical period or building type, but we have not tried to more than sketch a chronology of architectural history. A reader who wishes to know more about the history of architecture may consult our bibliography for books which treat history in more depth and give more examples of a particular historical period.

We have concentrated on the Western architectural traditions, but do not wish to imply that Eastern traditions are in any way inferior to those of the West. The East has a history of architecture as rich and brilliant as the West. Most of the concepts of architectural practice, of structure and of how architecture reveals the values of society will be new to the reader. We therefore decided to avoid the added complications of explaining the differences between Eastern and Western cultures that would be necessary if the reader is to understand the significance of many Eastern buildings. We hope that anyone reading our book will be sufficiently tantalized to discover the treasures of the East on his own.

Many new words and new meanings for familiar words will be encountered in the following pages: words which describe the materials and techniques used by architects; foreign names and customs; and critical terms used to analyze and describe buildings. These words will be explained in the text where practical. If an explanation seem to cause too much of a digression, the word is capitalized and explained in the glossary. Only words which cannot be found in a standard dictionary or those whose meaning in the jargon of the architect is significantly different from that found in a standard dictionary are explained.

We have underlined those words we think are most important to a basic, general, understanding of architecture and how it relates to society. We think that a reader who knows this vocabulary can be considered literate in architecture.

One final warning, architecture is addictive!

THE PRACTICE OF ARCHITECTURE

**GOD THE FATHER AS THE GREAT
ARCHITECT OF THE UNIVERSE**

The idea that the universe was designed in perfectly
geometrical patterns goes back to antiquity. Until the
late Renaissance, the Catholic Church maintained
that the universe was a series of concentric spheres
with the earth as the centermost and the orbits of
the sun and planets in the others. The diameters of
these spheres were related to each other by the har-
monic proportions of musical scales (thus the expression "the music of the spheres"). To make their buildings conform to the universe that God, the Great
Architect designed, architects used similar geometries and mathematic proportions in buildings, particularly churches. The discoveries of Galileo and other
astronomers forced the Church (and architects) to
reconsider their theories. The drawing to the left not
only illustrates the concept of the perfect universe it
also indicates the high esteem in which architects
were held during the Middle Ages.

drawing by William B. C. Harroff from an
illuminated French Bible of the 13th century.

> We shape our buildings, and then our buildings shape us.
>
> Sir Winston Churchill

Richard Neutra, a famous architect from California, used to maintain that he could either enhance the marriage of a couple or destroy it by the way he designed a house for them. Well, a house designed so the kitchen is so far from the dining room that the food always arrives cold or so the front door opens directly into the master bedroom might make life in the house a trial, but it's hard to imagine that these things would cause a divorce. The couple might legitimately curse the architect and sell or remodel the house, however.

Similarly, a German, Paul Scheerbart, argued just before the First World War that architecture could change the lives of the people living in it. He argued for an all-glass architecture. He couldn't conceive of anyone leading an evil life if they lived behind a glass wall. But we know that if one lives in a glass house and wants to do something evil, he merely has to pull the drapes.

If we can dismiss these two claims as trivial examples of architecture "shaping" the lives of individuals, of merely making life more or less comfortable and convenient, can we still say with Churchill that architecture affects our lives in any significant way?

Well, at one extreme, the skyscraper apartment buildings which have replaced more traditional neighborhoods of one and two story houses do affect people's lives in profound ways. The sidewalk and front porch of traditional neighborhoods have been replaced by the elevator, its lobby and dull corridors where no one lingers. The chance of residents in a skyscraper meeting any but their immediate neighbors has been reduced. The way society functions has been altered by how a building was designed.

More typically, the design of a building can make us feel either better or worse about whatever it is we are doing. For example, the architectural surroundings in a fine restaurant can contribute almost as much to the enjoyment of a meal as the way the food has been prepared and served.

But it is in the buildings that house those activities society thinks are most important that we really begin to appreciate what society expects architecture at its best to do for us.

Nearly every temple, mosque or church since time immemorial is more elaborate than it needs to be merely to provide a place for people to worship together. The major worship space of the church is probably much loftier than necessary; there may be marble coverings on walls and floors instead of asphalt tile; paintings or stained glass windows instead of bare walls and clear windows; elaborate chandeliers and carved seating; and towers and steeples on the outside which serve no earthly purpose. But the elaboration of the interior and the exterior serves an unearthly purpose. It says to everyone that we value our religion more than other institutions because we have lavished more attention on the buildings housing it.

We may be willing to accept the most economical sort of building for our factories and even for our businesses, but we usually do not for our churches. Most people feel the same way about our government buildings: the great dome on the Capitol of the United States is, functionally speaking, nearly useless. It was very expensive to build and costs a great deal to maintain -- but it serves as a symbol for the country and gives Americans a sense of pride and patriotism when they see it.

Government could be carried on in a factory, we can worship in a restaurant or work in our living room, but most activities are more effective, efficient and pleasurable when they take place in buildings designed specifically for them.

The creation of appropriate -- and beautiful or inspiring -- images, environments and symbols for people and their activities is one of the most exciting and glorious things an architect does, one of the things which separate him from other people. His success is one of the criteria with which we judge whether a building is bad, good or even great. But it is only one criterion.

The ancient Roman architect and writer Vitruvius wrote nearly 2000 years ago that there were three criteria for judging architecture, and despite some recent attempts to declare him old-fashioned, we haven't found anything better to replace them with:

Firmitas -- firmness: how a building stands up, that is, its structure

Utilitas -- commodity: how a building accommodates the activities for which it was designed, that is, how it functions

Venustas -- delight: how a building appeals to the aesthetic sense, that is, its beauty

The discussion so far as been concerned primarily with the last of the three criteria, the only one which is really controversial. Almost everyone would agree that buildings shouldn't fall down under normal circumstances and that, for example, the kitchen should be relatively close to the dining room, but people have vastly differing concepts of what beauty is or is not. Some modernists have questioned whether beauty is even important if a building is structurally sound and functions properly. Still, most people would agree that Vitruvius' third criterion does set something we call architecture (or even "Architecture") apart from mere building. We may argue about whether one piece of architecture is more beautiful than another or even whether a given example is beautiful at all, but Sir Nikolaus Pevsner's statement that "A bicycle shed is a building; Lincoln Cathedral is a piece of architecture" seems to make the proper distinction.

Even so, a building must not fall down on its inhabitants. It must stay up before we can discuss whether or not it is beautiful. The structure is the skeleton of a building; without it we can have no building, so we must take a brief look at the variety of systems an architect may use to structure a building before turning to other concerns. Structural engineering is a very technical field of study, but a few, simple, terms and concepts will give us a feeling for how a building stands.

STRUCTURAL SYSTEMS

SHEER MASS

The simplest sort of structure is created by piling up stones or brick or earth like the ancient Egyptians did in their pyramids or the American Indians did with their burial mounds. This type of structure can be very impressive but has limited value for living beings since there can be little space to move around in. Nevertheless, the structural materials, even in a pyramid built out of solid stone, must obey the most important force the architect or engineer must deal with: gravity. In a system of sheer mass, gravity tends to flatten the structure. The weight of the upper parts of the structure exerts a force on, presses on, compresses, the lower parts. This force, present in the supporting elements of all buildings is called compression.

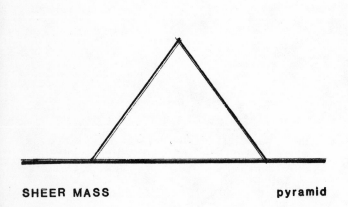

SHEER MASS   **pyramid**

TRABEATED SYSTEMS

(POST AND LINTEL) · (POST AND BEAM)

Somewhat more useful than a system of sheer mass, but nearly as simple, is the structure created by erecting two posts (for example two logs) and bridging between them with a third. The uprights are called posts or columns, the distance between them is called the span and the element they support is called a lintel or a beam. This, in its simplest form, is the trabeated system.

It will be useful later for our discussion to generalize the division of structural systems into two parts, the "carrier" (what does the holding up) and the "carried" (what is held up). In the trabeated system the posts are the carriers and the beam is the carried. The exact relationship between carrier and carried helps to distinguish the characteristics of a structural system. They are not always clearly distinguished. In a

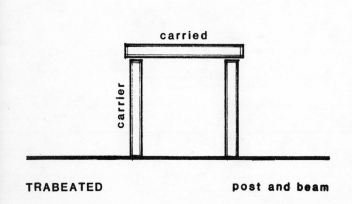

TRABEATED   **post and beam**

system of sheer mass, for example, the top stone is the only element which is merely carried, the other stones both carry and are carried.

Different periods of architecture can often be characterized by whether an architect chooses to express the structure of a building, whether he hides the the carrier and carried inside a wall or clearly shows them on the outside or inside. He may, for example, make one system of carrier and carried appear to hold up a building when in fact another system actually does. We will encounter all of these approaches.

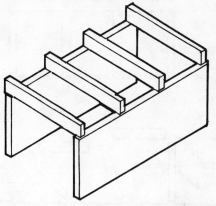

BEARING WALL

A beam <u>bears</u> (rests) on its supports. If the support, the carrier, is a wall instead of a column, that wall is consequently called a <u>bearing wall</u>. If the carrier is relatively small, such as in a building supported on columns (like a gothic cathedral or a skyscraper), the columns are <u>point supports</u> and the building is said to be <u>point supported</u>.

The weight of the beam presses down on the columns, post or wall. If the supports are vertical, there are only compression forces in them. It's a bit more complicated for the beam, however. You can imagine what goes on by visualizing a beam which is thinner than it ought to be. Common sense will tell you that the beam will sag in the middle. Now imagine the beam at the sag. Its top would start to wrinkle; there would be a squeezing effect there, so we can say the top of the beam is in compression. Its bottom would be pulled apart, stretched. This stretching force is called <u>tension</u>.

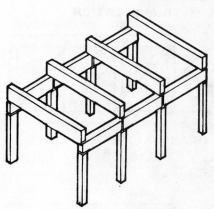

POINT SUPPORT

compression

tension

It's important for the architect to know what forces are working in his building and what materials are best for each force. For example, stone is very strong in compression but very weak in tension. So if he builds a trabeated building with stone, he doesn't have to worry much about the columns, but he cannot allow the beams to sag; too much tension will cause the beam to crack and fall. He must therefore either keep the spans small or make the beams deeper (thicker) to reduce tension in them.

Until materials like steel, which is quite strong in tension, were developed, the trabeated system imposed limits on building. As a beam gets deeper and heavier in order to span larger spaces, it weighs more and the columns must be made thicker to withstand compression. In large buildings, much of the floor space eventually gets taken up by the columns.

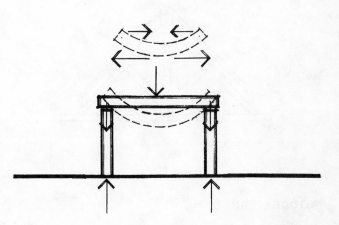

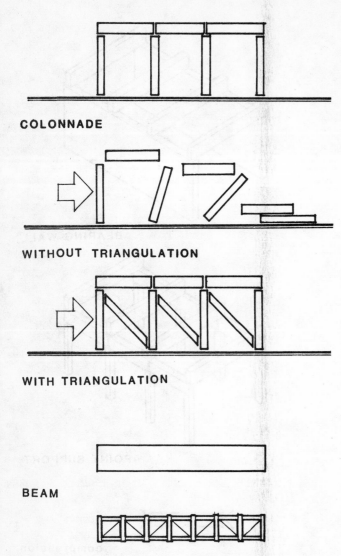

COLONNADE

WITHOUT TRIANGULATION

WITH TRIANGULATION

BEAM

TRUSS

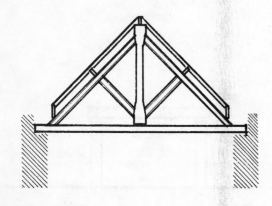

WOODEN TRUSS

Besides, there is a limit to how deep a beam can practically be made before it collapses under its own weight or exceeds the size of materials available. In any case, the optimal spacing of supports and dimensions of a beam involves fairly complicated calculations. Modern engineers can make them, but the ancients had only trial and error to figure out these sizes. No doubt lots of their buildings collapsed with unpleasant results for both inhabitants and builders.

A line of columns which are continuously connected by a series of beams is called a colonnade. Although it is a very simple device (and sometimes necessary to build big buildings) it is a particularly attractive one which architects discovered very early and still use today.

A trabeated system produces a useful, rectangular, space between the posts and lintels, but the rectangular shape of this construction is not very stable if something pushes sideways on it. It has a nasty tendency to change into a lozenge shape and fall down (as anyone who has home-made bookshelves knows). But a third support which goes from the foot of one post to the top of the other divides the rectangle into two triangles (triangulation), and since a triangle cannot change shape without the sides being broken or deformed, the resulting structure is as strong as the elements or members which make it up.

Triangulation can be used to minimize some of the problems associated with the trabeated system, for example the heavy, deep, beams associated with long spans. You've seen it used in bridges, which are often just beams with a road on top of them. Where a solid beam would be too deep to be practical, it may be replaced by an assembly of much smaller beams and rods which are arranged in a continuous series of triangles. This assembly is called a truss. It may be used in place of beams in many locations besides bridges. Some of the members (the rods or beams which form the sides of the small triangles) will be in tension, others in compression. It takes an expert to know what size to make each of these members, especially in large trusses. But a truss can be much lighter than the beam it replaces, and whereas a beam normally has to be made of one continuous piece of material (a single log, for example), a truss can be made of many smaller (and cheaper) pieces.

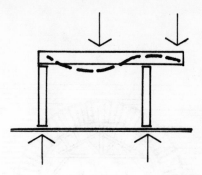

CANTILEVER

If a beam extends past its support, the overhang is called a <u>cantilever</u>. There are many reasons for using a cantilever. An architect might use it to make a building look more interesting; or he might extend the beams of a floor out to make a deck or a balcony; or ceiling beams can be cantilevered to make a canopy which shades the house. As long as a beam isn't cantilevered too far, the tendency of the end of the cantilever to droop will counteract the tendency of the center of the beam to sag, thus a cantilevered beam can be shallower than one that isn't.

There is a special sort of cantilever which can be used with small pieces of material -- bricks or blocks of stones, for example. If these pieces are assembled in layers, and the last piece in each row is cantilevered just a little over the one below it, the whole assemblage can be projected quite a distance. You may have piled up building blocks this way as children. The small cantilevers are called <u>corbels</u>. If an opening is spanned by corbelling from the two supports toward the center, the triangular-shaped opening is called a <u>corbel arch</u>. This is a useful technique in areas where there aren't big enough pieces of materials to make beams or enough expertise to design trusses. The corbel has its limitations also, and in ancient times man discovered how to replace it with a far more versatile technique, the true <u>arch</u>.

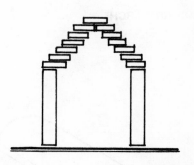

CORBEL ARCH

ARCUATED SYSTEMS

Let's consider a MASONRY arch. It might be described as a curved beam made of a series of trapezoidal, wedge-shaped, blocks called <u>voussoirs</u>. The voussoir in the center of the arch is called a <u>keystone</u>. You can understand how an arch works by starting with the keystone. Gravity tries to pull it straight down, but it is wedged between the voussoirs on either side. Each succeeding voussoir is likewise wedged between those to either side. Gravity wants the force or <u>thrust</u> which each one exerts on the next to be directed straight down, but the sloping face of the voussoirs directs it at a diagonal. The thrusts of the voussoirs add up arithmetically, so that the total thrust exerted on each support is fairly great -- and pushes on it at an angle, not straight down like a beam. The supports themselves -- walls or columns -- must be very thick to keep from being overturned. Alternatively, arches may be placed next to each other forming an <u>arcade</u>. In an arcade the overturning forces of one arch are balanced by those

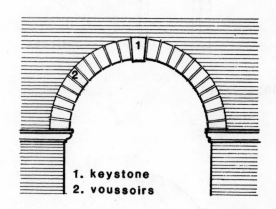

1. keystone
2. voussoirs

MASONRY ARCH   **ARCUATED**

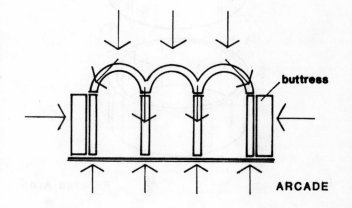

buttress

ARCADE

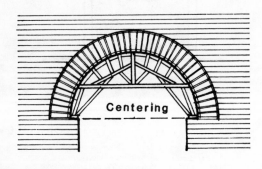

ROMAN MASONRY ARCH

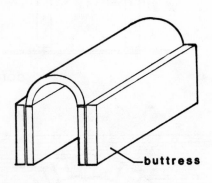

BARREL VAULT

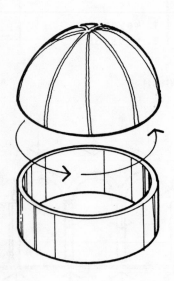

DOME   **Rotated Arch**

in the arch next to it and the thrust is directed straight down. The end arch in an arcade must be well supported or the whole series will fall down like a row of dominoes. The diagonal thrusts in an arch are always present; an arch is always trying to fall down. "An arch never sleeps". But if an arch is well-designed, every piece of it is in compression. That means an architect may use small pieces of materials which are not strong in resisting tension, like stone or brick, to build an arch, and if he can contain the final thrusts an arch exerts on its supports, he can build it almost any size he wishes.

The advantages of the arcuated over the trabeated system are obvious then: potentially great spans using small pieces of materials. But besides containing the sleepless thrusting of the arch, the architect must take into account its limitations. Until the keystone is in place, an arch will fall down. It must be temporarily supported by centering (usually made of wood) which is the exact shape of the underside of the arch. The centering is removed once the keystone is in place and the supports for the arch sufficiently sturdy. Centering takes a great deal of skill to construct. So do the voussoirs. Each one must be carefully and individually shaped. In the end, an arcuated system usually demands more skilled labor than a trabeated system. It is, however, usually worth the extra trouble if building materials are expensive; if sufficiently large beams can't be found or if the labor is non-union. Cultures (like the ancient Roman Empire) with a good supply of skilled slaves are often fond of arcuated systems.

The arcuated system is quite versatile, especially in its more elaborate forms. For example if an arch spanning between two parallel walls is, in effect, slid along the tops of the walls it forms a shape which resembles half of a tube split lengthways, half of a barrel. This sort of longitudinal arch is called a barrel VAULT. If the arch spans across a supporting wall which is curved into a circle, and the arch is, in effect rotated around the circle, a special VAULT resembling half of a ping-pong ball is formed. This is called a dome. Both of these types of vaults (and there are many others) exert outward thrusts which try to overturn the walls (or columns) on which they sit just like the arch from which they are derived. Either the walls must be very thick or smaller supporting walls, called buttresses, must be built to counter the thrusts.

SHELL STRUCTURES

Most vaults based on the principle of the arch are fairly thick and built of relatively small units of MASONRY. An architect or engineer who fully understands how forces are distributed in a vault may use a material such as REINFORCED CONCRETE, which is very strong both in tension and compression, to design structures based on the principle of the egg shell. If a membrane, like the shell of the egg, is curved or folded properly it can be made extremely thin and still hold itself up. Then large spaces such as convention halls can be made using relatively small amounts of materials. The system is too complicated to explain here, requires clever engineering and very careful construction, but the savings in the amount of materials needed to produce a structure can sometimes make shell structures desirable.

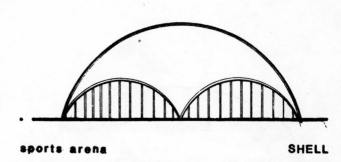

sports arena   SHELL

TENSILE STRUCTURES

Consider a piece of rope tied around the branch of a tree. If you swing on the rope, gravity will pull on you and pull the rope taut. It is in pure tension. Even a relatively thin rope will hold you up. But if you try to use the rope as a column, putting the same rope in compression, it will not even be able to hold up its own weight. The rope would have to be made immensely thick to hold you up. It is obvious, then, that it takes relatively little of materials which are very good at resisting tensile forces (like steel and some plastics) to hold up immense weights. A suspension bridge is a good example of a tensile structure. The cables holding the roadway are hung from huge PYLONS, and although the PYLONS must withstand a great deal of compression, the cables spanning the river are in tension and can be exquisitely thin. A beam, or even a truss, which could span the same distance would be gargantuan. Roofs of buildings can also be hung from vertical supports and be made relatively thin. There are even some tall buildings whose floors are hung from a central support rather than supported by columns.

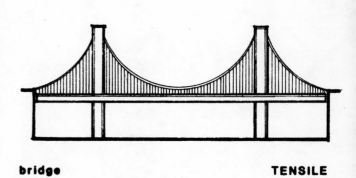

bridge   TENSILE

AIR-SUPPORTED STRUCTURES

A new type of structure which has been developed in recent years makes use of some of the principles of the membrane seen in shell structures and some of the principles of tensile structures -- and is inspired by the common balloon. The rubber membrane of a balloon is a material which stretches, is strong in tension, very lightweight, and can enclose a large volume (relative to the thickness of the enclosing membrane). The air which is pumped into the balloon stretches the membrane but is held in and compressed by it. Curiously air, which normally has no compressive strength, becomes a structural element when held in place by the tensile forces in the balloon membrane. The idea can be extended to the size of a building and is frequently used to cover outdoor swimming pools and some large sports stadiums. A pump must continually be used to keep up the pressure inside the air supported structure. If the pump stops, the whole structure deflates. But when this happens, the building collapses in slow motion, giving people time to get out -- which is not the case with other types of structures when they fall down.

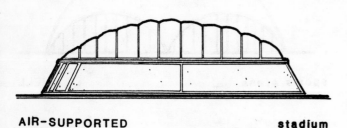

AIR-SUPPORTED   **stadium**

We have listed the major structural systems available to architects in order of increasing complexity. This is generally the order in which they were developed historically. The modern architect and engineer have the full range of these systems and new construction materials and techniques that have been developed in the last century at their disposal. The choice of which structure is most economical, practical and aesthetically appropriate for a given building has become immensely complex, too complex for most architects to make by themselves. They need the assistance of an engineer who specializes in architectural structures. Perhaps in the distant beginnings of architecture, one man may have been able to know enough to design a building by himself; but in the 20th century architecture is almost always a team sport. The architect is more like a quarterback or the conductor of an orchestra than a solo performer.

THE DESIGN PROCESS

> Architecture cannot be the world's oldest profession -- tradition has decided that issue long ago -- but its antiquity is not in doubt.
>
> Spiro Kostof

Imhotep, the first architect known by name, lived and worked more than 3,600 years ago in ancient Egypt. He was brilliant. He conceived the first monumental, stone building known to man. He was also very successful: he was made a god by the ancient Egyptians. This hasn't happened since then, a fact which might surprise some architects.

Imhotep would recognize some of the things an architect does today -- especially in the early stages of designing a building -- but much of the modern architect's duties would be new to him. Like the modern architect, he would have had a client, the person who commands or commissions the building. Both architects would probably help the client decide where to place the building (site selection); both would find the best and worst qualities of the site (site analysis): views to and from the site, what effect sun and wind will have, the slope of the land, the character of other buildings around the site and so forth. Both would help the client to prepare a program, a description of what functions the building needs to accommodate, how these functions relate to each other, and how big the different areas accommodating the functions will have to be. Both the ancient and the modern architect would prepare one or more concepts, general ideas of how the building should look, how the requirements set out in the program are functionally organized and given visual form. Both architects would probably also decide how the smaller parts of the building should go together (the details) and would give some sort of directions to the workmen to make the building look as the architect imagined it. Both might visit the site to make sure the workmen were following instructions (project supervision).

We have already described more duties than one man can manage, even a god like Imhotep, if a building is much larger than a small house. Even he probably had assistants. Most modern buildings are much more complicated than those faced by Imhotep. For example, they have complicated systems for heating, cooling, ventilating and lighting the building, and the architect is responsible for determining the size and location of every furnace and air-conditioning unit, of every light and light switch, of every toilet and sink as well as every beam and wall. A special engineer must assist the architect in designing and integrating these systems into his building. He may also have to consult a specialist in acoustics or land-scaping or kitchen planning or a specialist in interior furnishings. The list of these people, called consultants, who have specialized knowledge the architect does not have enough time to acquire, can be very long. The cost of the services and equipment they provide may account for the major part of the total cost of a building.

Imhotep may have been able to direct the construction of his buildings by verbal instructions to the workmen, some small models, and a few drawings. Because of the complex nature of buildings today and for legal reasons, the modern architect must prepare an elaborate set of drawings and written descriptions to get a building constructed. After his concept is approved by the client, he prepares a somewhat more detailed schematic design. This, as the name suggests, is a sort of an outline of how the building will look and where the major functions are to be located. If the schematic design is approved by the client, it is developed in more detail (design development). The subtopics of the outline are, as it were, filled in. When the client gives final approval to these design development drawings, the building can be "written" from the outline. The offices of the architect and his consultants prepare production drawings (which are also called working drawings or blueprints) which show the appearance, size and location of everything in the completed building.

The architect uses several types of drawings to study and explain the building he is designing. To study functional relations (where the dining room is located with respect to the kitchen, the living room and the front door, for examples) he draws plans. Plans are two-dimensional (that is, they give no sense of depth) drawings which show horizontal relationships. It is as if the building were sliced horizontally a few feet off the floor and you were looking down on it.

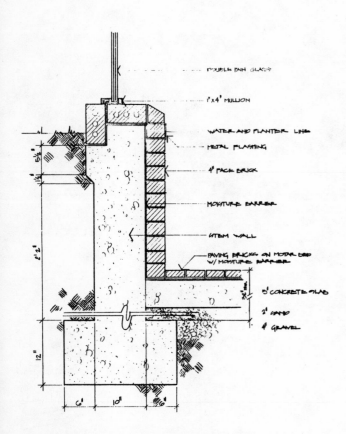

DOUBLE PAIN GLASS

1'x4' MULLION

WATER AND PLANTER LINE

METAL FLASHING

4' FACE BRICK

MOISTURE BARRIER

STEM WALL

PAVING BRICKS ON MORTAR BED W/ MOISTURE BARRIER

5' CONCRETE SLAB

2' SAND

4' GRAVEL

ARCHITECTURAL WORKING DRAWING

To study the heights of the various rooms and the relationships between floors (and to make sure people don't bump their heads on the ceilings when they walk up stairs) the architect draws sections. Sections (or cross-sections) are also two-dimensional representations of the building, but they show vertical relationships. It is as if a huge knife sliced straight down through a building, the part in front of the knife-cut was removed and you looked at the cut building head on.

To study the exterior faces of the building, the facades, the architect draws elevations. These are two-dimensional drawings which show the sizes, shapes and relationships of doors, windows and other elements on the exterior of a building. Elevations may also give an indication of what materials are going to be used on the exterior of a building.

Most of these drawings must be done smaller than the actual size of the room or building element they represent, but they are always done so that the length of every line on the drawing is done to the same arithmetic fraction of the true length of the line it represents. Architects call this making a drawing to scale. For example, in a plan done to a scale of 1/16 inch = 1 foot, a line on the drawing 1/16 of an inch long represents a distance of one foot in the actual building.

Since none of these drawings give an impression of depth or volume, of how we normally see a building, an architect may also make perspectives. These drawings use techniques developed to give an illusion of depth on a flat surface. They are often colored, with trees, people, furniture and shadows represented and can look almost like a photograph of the finished building. Perspectives are drawn of both the interior and exterior of buildings. Some architects also like to build models which can give an even more realistic idea of how the finished building will look. Models, like plans, sections and elevations are usually done to some specified scale. Perspectives are not.

Along with the working drawings, the architect prepares a written document called the specifications. It describes things which are difficult to show in drawings: the quality of materials used in construction, methods of construction and the minimal acceptable standards of materials and equipment used in the building.

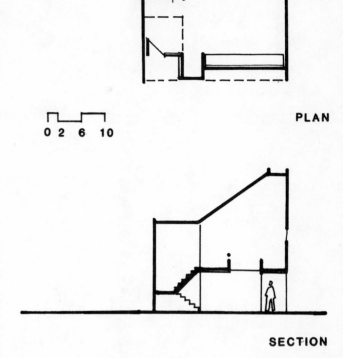

0 2 6 10

PLAN

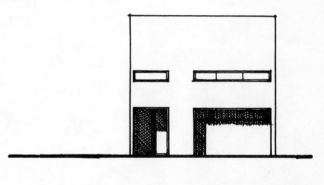

SECTION

FRONT ELEVATION

PERSPECTIVE

In many cases, the architect is required to see that the building is constructed exactly according to the working drawings and specifications (project super-vision). Good architects usually visit their buildings after completion to see and learn from what has worked well and what hasn't (project follow-up).

Most architects enjoy their jobs very much. It is exciting to conceive a building and see it built. But most also need to earn a living and consequently must charge the client for the fun they have. The client must pay a fee to the architect for each step of the design and building process outlined above. There is a separate fee assessed for developing the program for a project, for developing the concept, for design development drawings, for working draw-ings and for supervising the construction of a buil-ding. In practice, the architect often sets a single fee which covers all these phases. The fee is usually based upon a percentage of the total cost of the building (it may vary from about 2% to more than 10% depending on the services requested and the type of building). If the client decides not to build after the working drawings are prepared, he is still (generally) required to pay the architect for all services completed to that point.

From the fee the client pays him, the architect must pay all the engineers and other consultants needed in designing the client's building and the assistants (other architects and draftsmen) to prepare the mul-titude of schematic, design development and working drawings. In a large architectural firm there may be more than a thousand draftsmen working for the architects who own it. Even though the fee an architect charges may seem huge to the client, it is divided up among many people. Surprisingly little remains for the architect himself.

Does the client really get his money's worth for the fee charged by an architect? Why should anyone hire an architect, anyway? Well, one good reason is that in most states and countries you have to hire an architect if you're building anything bigger than a house. It's the law. And that law exists to protect the public. It requires that buildings are designed by someone who has enough knowledge and experience to see that all parts of the building are strong enough to keep the building from falling down under normal circumstances (which in some parts of the country may include earthquakes); that the building has been designed to resist fire and storm; that the

plumbing is sanitary; that the building will be sufficiently heated and ventilated; and that it meets
similar rules (building codes) established by the city,
county and state to assure the safety of the public.

Not everyone may call himself an architect and claim
that he has the knowledge necessary to assure the
building he designs meets all codes. Only someone
who is licensed by the state in which he practices
may legally call himself an architect and prepare
drawings for public buildings. It is as difficult and
demanding to get a license to practice architecture
as it is to practice medicine. Typically, a licensed
architect has completed 5 rigorous years of training
in a university which has been approved by a national
group of architects. He must also work for three
years as an apprentice in an architect's office. Only
then may he take an examination which lasts 4 days.
If he passes this exam (and even after 8 years of
study, the majority do not pass this difficult exam
the first time they take it) he may call himself an
architect.

In short the client is paying for someone with the
expertise and experience necessary to take legal
responsibility for constructing a public building. In
addition the client is paying for an impartial, objective observer to arbitrate any problems associated
with construction -- and this sort of problem, unanti-
cipated by the inexperienced client, usually causes
the greatest headaches in building and often significant cost overruns. A good and vigilant architect
may earn his fees from the client's point of view in
this stage of the design process alone.

The most subjective, but perhaps the unique, service
rendered by the architect to the client is his ability
to solve difficult problems creatively. The non-
architect tends to settle upon the first solution that
seems reasonable, and that solution will most likely
be based on examples of similar buildings known to
him. If the example happens to be a good one and
relatively close to the type of building being
designed, the result may be excellent. Many fine
houses, barns and the like have been designed by
non-architects. This type of architecture, not
designed by trained architects and based on local
traditions, is called vernacular architecture. There
are many superb examples all over the world equal in
quality to the best work done by architects.

If the building to be designed is functionally or tech-nically complicated or of a type for which there are no good precedents, a solution by a non-architect may be less than successful. The architect has been trained both to profit from precedent (of which he will have a wider knowledge than the non-architect) and to solve problems from scratch, abstracting experience from apparently dissimilar situations to the problem at hand. He will attempt several solutions to the building problem posed by the client, approaching the solutions from as many ways as he can think of, then develop the best of them to show the client. Because of his experience and training, he is usually aware of more things which affect the problem and its solution than the non-architect. And a good architect attempts to find an excellent func-tional solution which is <u>simultaneously</u> within the budget of the client, structurally sound and aes-thetically appealing. <u>Firmness, Commodity and Delight</u>!

One can, in some ways, liken the role of an architect to that of a doctor. One hardly goes to a doctor for every cold or small injury. Home remedies do nicely -- perhaps as well as those the doctor could offer. But when a disease or injury appears serious or could become serious, most people turn to a specialist for help. Even simple flu can turn into pneumonia. Unfor-tunately, just as some doctors are less than competent, some architects are quacks. There are several ways to find good architects. Look for recently completed buildings you like and find out who was the architect. Most architects keep photo-graphs of their buildings in their offices. Visit several architects and look through their collections of photographs (called portfolios or brochures). Talk to other people who have commissioned buildings from architects. This will give you an opportunity to find out if the architect really does search for a variety of solutions, if he is thorough in his inspection of the building while it is constructed, and so forth.

A special procedure is sometimes used to find an out-standing design if the structure is especially impor-tant. A contest, called a <u>competition</u> is staged between architects. The client may open the compe-tition to a broad group or may limit the entrants only to those the client and his advisors select. A jury composed of the client, architects not entering the competitions and others votes on the best design. Normally, prize money is given to the winner and the runners up, and the winner is given the commission for the building. Thus, the client pays for the competition and prizes in addition to the architect's fee, but in principle he gets the best possible building and the best value for his budget. The White House, the Capitol and the recent Vietnam Veteran's Memorial in Washington, D.C., were all the result of competitions.

Up to this point, you may have gotten the impression from what we've written that the architect's client is the person who uses the building designed for him. The last examples show this is not always true, and it is an important point for you to remember. For example the client who commissioned the White House never used it. In this case the client was not even a single person but rather representatives of "the American people" The user is the President (and, in a sense, the American people, too). You are part of the "client" in all public building and in most cases have the right to be part of the review aspect of the design process by way of hearings, design review boards, committees who write building codes, and so forth.

There are other examples where the client is not the user of a building. A client may commission an apartment building or an office building without ever entering it. In these cases, too, the architect as a professional serves a useful function. He represents the unknown user as well as the client. The typical non-architect would feel much less constrained to do that.

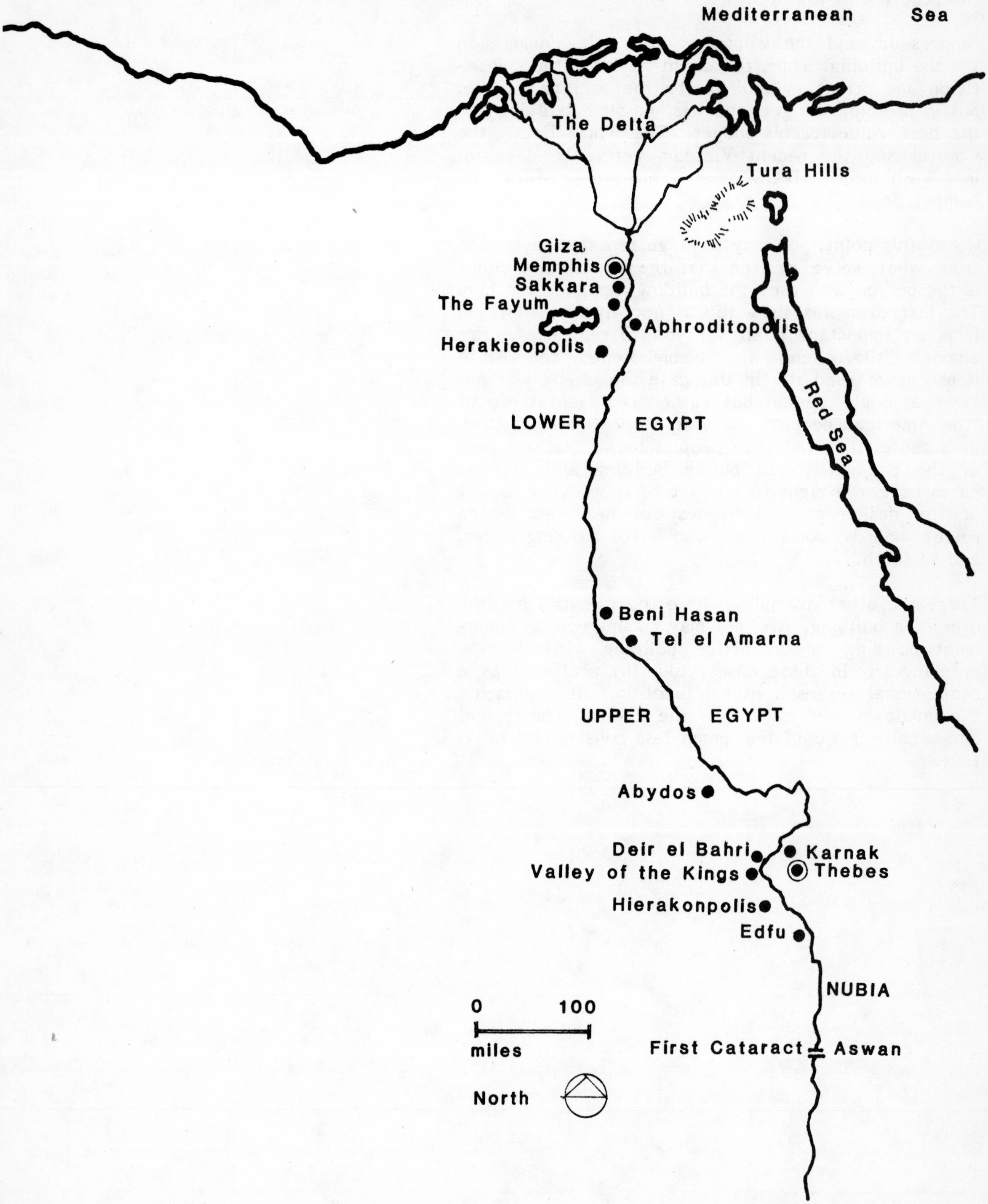

Mediterranean   Sea

The Delta

Tura Hills

Giza
Memphis
Sakkara
The Fayum
Aphroditopolis
Herakieopolis

Red Sea

LOWER   EGYPT

Beni Hasan
Tel el Amarna

UPPER   EGYPT

Abydos

Deir el Bahri
Valley of the Kings
Karnak
Thebes
Hierakonpolis
Edfu

NUBIA

0   100

miles

North

First Cataract — Aswan

ARCHITECTURE OF THE ANCIENT WORLD

MAP OF ANCIENT EGYPT

Egypt consisted of an extremely narrow strip of fertile land on either side of the Nile River and a triangular Delta where the Nile flowed into the Mediterranean Sea. Beyond the fertile land was trackless desert. This geography naturally divided Egypt into two parts: Lower Egypt (the Delta region) and Upper Egypt (the area along the Nile to the south of the Delta). These two parts were united into one country in Prehistoric times by the legendary King Narmer. The desert was a natural barrier to enemies and permitted Egyptian culture to develop in relative isolation.

PREHISTORY

The other arts are older than architecture. Painting, sculpture and the decorative arts are found in caves like Lascaux in France or Altamira in Spain. These cave men were hunter-gatherers who moved around with the supply of game, fruits and nuts and needed only the most rudimentary sort of shelter. They maintained locations with common religious significance, but caves were perfectly suitable for cultures with little leisure time for building.

Architecture awaited the development of agrarian societies. Agriculture ties societies to a specific location, and a localized society cannot escape some form of governmental organization and the structures which house and symbolize it: administrative and religious buildings, storage and defense structures.

Architecture, unlike painting and sculpture, is the art of civilization; the art of urban cultures. It concretizes living patterns. Not only do buildings indicate what a society thought was worth expending time and effort to make permanent, but also their very existence tends to perpetuate the patterns which brought them into being in the first place. Inevitably, the existence of a "palace" for the ruler indicates to the outside that a culture is established and to the culture itself the status of the ruler. Architecture is fundamentally the art of the establishment.

The caveman artists at Lascaux and Altamira were as intelligent and talented as anyone from the succeeding 15,000 years or so, yet they appear not to have lived in buildings much less in cities. Why then, did towns and cities -- and consequently architecture -- "suddenly" come into existence after the millennia that intelligent man existed without them. That remains an intriguing question, although there are many theories.

The first permanent settlements, at least in the West, seem to have been farming communities established in Mesopotamia (modern Iraq) and the land surrounding it. The foundations of the Biblical city of Jericho date back at least 9,000 years to around 7,000 B. C. There were probably farming communities in Egypt nearly as old. Some people believe these

cave painting   LASCAUX

towns emerged as the result of Divine intervention. Most scientists think that climatic changes transformed a lush, sub-tropical region into a semi-arid region and man was forced to cultivate his own food to survive. Whichever was the case, the plow and irrigation were developed, agriculture was made possible and urban society began.

The first towns were city-states, small, independent groups of people living together so that they may cooperate on projects too elaborate for a family but necessary for agriculture: mutual defense, an irrigation system, harvesting and marketing of crops. The members of the community must specialize to some extent. A few may produce pottery for the community, others hunt, others farm and so on. This is a more efficient way of life than hunting-gathering and allows some people enough leisure time to elaborate the purely utilitarian; to decorate pottery, for example, or make buildings beautiful as well as functional; to create art. It is also worth noting that all societies well enough organized to have leisure time seem to have created art. The desire to make things attractive seems to be part of human nature.

Only fairly large cultures have the resources in time and money necessary to create large, elaborate buildings, however. Monumental architecture with artistic pretensions depended upon the emergence of a more complex culture than the city-state.

EGYPTIAN ARCHITECTURE

Egypt has fascinated mankind for several thousand years. Its curious religion, art and architecture has inspired some bizarre stories in an attempt to explain them: Jewish slaves toiling under cruel taskmasters to build the pyramid; mummies, corpses wrapped in strips of linen, sightlessly stalking archeologists; creepy tombs filled with gold, jewels, and inscriptions which contain the wisdom of the ages. These stories were not entirely created by Hollywood for the midnight horror movies, however. Many were old before the time of Christ, attempts to explain a culture which was already incredibly ancient 2000 years ago. People had forgotten how to read its picture-writings, called hieroglyphics (sacred writing) by the

Greeks. During the last 200 years, archeologists have uncovered many documents and artifacts of ancient Egypt, beautifully preserved by its dry climate. We now know how to read hieroglyphics. Ironically, we know more about what the ancient Egyptians believed and about how and why the pyramids and tombs were built than an Egyptian who lived 2000 years ago.

The culture of ancient Egypt existed nearly 3000 years without significant change, from about 3100 B. C. to its conquest by Alexander the Great in 323 B. C. It was an incredibly stable society if we compare it to the changes which have taken place in the last 2000 years. The West has seen the Roman soldier give way to the knights and castles of the Middle Ages and the knight in armor to the space-suited astronaut on the moon. Egyptian culture changed so little that only someone quite familiar with Egyptian art can tell whether a painting or sculpture was created at the beginning of the 3000 year culture or the end. Those changes in social structure which did occur are somewhat easier to follow in its architecture.

The Prehistoric city-states grouped themselves loosely into two geographic confederations. Lower Egypt, the area to the north of Egypt roughly corresponding to the delta of the Nile River, and Upper Egypt, the area along the Nile to the south of the delta. About 3100 years before Christ, the leader of a wealthy trading and pottery manufacturing town in Upper Egypt, a man known in Egyptian legend as King Narmer, conquered all of Upper and Lower Egypt. He created the first national state.

Power was inherited, in ancient Egypt, by the oldest female in a family, who transferred it to the man she married. He became king or PHARAOH. A family or dynasty retained power until it died out or was conquered by a different family group. There were a total of 30 dynasties in ancient Egypt.

After Narmer, dynasty followed dynasty for over 850 years (the Old Kingdom). Then a series of civil disorders (the First Intermediate Period) sent Egypt into chaos. Order was gradually restored during several dynasties called the Middle Kingdom. Egypt, which had previously been protected from invasion by the deserts on three sides and the Mediterranean Sea on the other, was finally conquered by mysterious outsiders. A Second Intermediate Period occurred. Eventually native Egyptian soldiers drove the foreigners out and re-established a culture almost indistinguishable in many aspects from a thousand years earlier. This new series of dynasties, called the New Kingdom or Empire, was different from the others in one, major, respect: the armies not only drove out the invaders, they also conquered surrounding countries. Egypt became an Empire and the army an important force in Egyptian society. The conquests brought immense wealth and, for the first time, slaves.

The PYRAMID was the characteristic architectural monument of the Old Kingdom. The first pyramid, the first monumental stone construction built by man, was constructed at Saqqara, just south of Memphis, capital of the Old Kingdom. It was the tomb of the pharaoh Zoser.

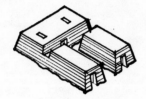

MASTABA

Zoser's Step Pyramid was designed by Imhotep, the first architect known by name. It is not a true pyramid with smoothly sloping sides, nor did Imhotep first conceive it in the form we see today. He first constructed a large mastaba, the traditional low, rectangular structure of solid stone and sloping sides which marked Egyptian graves. He next enlarged the mastaba to make it more impressive and then hit upon the brilliant idea of stacking successively smaller mastabas to create a sort of stairway to heaven over the subterranean burial chamber of the pharaoh. The final structure is immense -- as tall as a modern 18 story skyscraper -- but was only part of a COMPLEX of buildings, a sort of translation into stone of Zoser's mud-brick and wood palace at Memphis. This elaborate preparation for life after death reflected the Egyptians' religious beliefs.

STEP PYRAMID

They believed that life after death was eternal and would be pretty much like the brief existence on earth, a sort of preparatory phase. Tombs were for them their real, eternal, houses and should be stocked with all the things which the ka, the soul, enjoyed on earth. Symbols, such as paintings of beloved activities, were as valid for the soul as the real things, so Egyptian tombs are cheerful -- filled with all the delightful things of life -- not lugubrious.

The Step Pyramid set the standard for succeeding pharaohs, but the type was gradually modified. At Meidum, the builders started with a step pyramid but later encased it with stone so that the sides were smooth. They created the first true pyramid. It had serious structural flaws, however, and collapsed. The next several pyramids were more conservatively constructed. Architects gradually gained enough ex-

GREAT PYRAMID

perience and felt confident enough to build the <u>Great Pyramid</u> at Gizeh.

The Great Pyramid was built for the most powerful of the Old Kingdom pharaohs, <u>Khufu</u> (Cheops in Greek). It is an architectural masterpiece. This largest of the pyramids was conceived from the beginning as a true pyramid. It is of a size (as tall as a 45 story skyscraper) and was constructed with an accuracy that is still impressive by modern standards.

Through the ages people have attached mystical powers to the Great Pyramid; some think that its builders must have had extra-terrestrial help. It is really no more -- nor less -- than the summit of centuries of experience with pyramid building: the Egyptians had enough technology to build it. The people who suspect assistance from some superior culture fail to appreciate what large numbers of people working intelligently, if very slowly, can accomplish It is very likely that the pyramids were intended to be very labor-intensive in order to occupy peasants when they were idled by the annual flooding of the Nile. Although existing records show that at least some of the more skilled workmen were paid, building a pyramid was a religious act for most of them: they believed that the pharaoh was a god even while he lived on earth and that his tomb would be his eternal palace. The pyramids were not built by spacemen or slaves, and the Jewish peoples had nothing to do with the the pyramids since they were constructed at least 1000 years before the events described in the Old Testament.

The pyramid was only the most impressive part of a complex of buildings, marking the burial chamber of the king (usually below the pyramid, but sometimes within the pyramid itself). First there was a temple on the bank of the Nile where the king's body would be landed from the sacred barge; next a causeway would lead up to another temple at the base of the pyramid where the body would lie in state before it was interred and where the king would be worshipped for eternity (in principle). Unfortunately, the pyramids were supremely unsuccessful in protecting the remains and possessions of the pharaohs. By the New Kingdom they had all been robbed. For all practical purposes, pyramid building ended with the Old Kingdom.

The architecture of the Middle Kingdom was very low keyed. Its pharaohs were much less powerful than

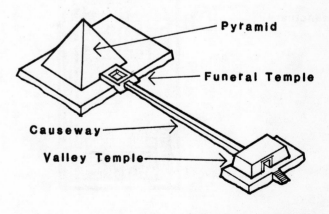

PYRAMID COMPLEX

their predecessors and in any case did not want to build such conspicuous advertisements for graverobbers as pyramids. They began a tradition of carving tombs out of solid, living, rock (rock-cut tombs) and locating the memorial temples elsewhere. These tombs could be elaborate on the inside but hidden from all but the ka on the exterior.

The New Kingdom moved the capital to Thebes in Upper Egypt, a more central location which offered greater protection from invasion. It was the site of the largest group of religious buildings ever built by man, chief among them the Temple of Amon-Re at Karnak. This city/temple/fortress/palace covered an area as large as mid-Manhattan and counted 86,000 slaves among its inhabitants. This and other temples are as characteristic of the visible architecture of the New Kingdom as the pyramids were of the Old. We may safely deduce from this that the pharaoh was no longer all-powerful. He had to share power to some degree with the priests (and, for that matter, the army).

The typical temple was composed of 7 parts which were arranged along a processional axis:

1. a landing on the Nile for the barge carrying a statue of the god

2. a processional avenue of SPHINXES from the landing to the temple proper

3. a pair of huge PYLONS with sculptured reliefs, flagpoles and colossal statues of the king

4. an entry court (usually colonnaded)

5. a hypostyle hall, a high room filled with closely-spaced columns, usually lit only by windows placed high in the outer walls (clerestory lighting)

6. a barge chamber for the sacred barge

7. a sanctuary for the statue of the god or gods; the "holy of holies"

Spaces along this processional axis became successively more enclosed and darker. The floor level rose, the ceiling dropped lower and lower, and the walls got closer together. As the spaces became more confined, admission was restricted until only pharaoh and

nile

nile landing

avenue of the sphinxes

pylon

Processional axis

Pylon Gate

Hypostyle Hall

barge chamber

sanctuary

TEMPLE of AMON-RE   **plan**

high priest were admitted to the sanctuary. This sequence of architectural spaces still has a powerful effect on a visitor even though the temples are in ruins.

The tradition of separating the memorial temple from a hidden, rock-cut tomb which had begun in the Middle Kingdom was carried on in the New. Both tomb and temple, the only visible memorial to a pharaoh, were built as a city of the dead on the river bank opposite Thebes, the city of the living. Tombs were hidden in the Valleys of the Kings and Queens, temples were built nearer the river. The most beautiful of these was built for the only female pharaoh, Queen Hatshepsut. Her architect was her **very** dear friend Senmut. They built an exquisite structure of colonnaded, landscaped, terraces stacked against a sheer cliff. The horizontals of the terraces and the closely spaced columns beautifully reflect the rock formations behind them. The following centuries produced larger and more imposing temples, but none to match the calm beauty of Hatshepsut's valley temple.

hypostyle section   TEMPLE OF AMON-RE

MINOAN ARCHITECTURE

The Minoan culture flourished on the Mediterranean island of Crete from about 2000-1159 B. C. Greek myth spoke of a King Minos (after whom the culture is named) and his fabulous palace. His wife Pasiphae had an affair with a bull that resulted in the Minotaur. Somewhat embarrassed, Minos commissioned his architect Daedalus to build a labyrinth, a maze-like structure, for the creature. Most modern scholars doubted the story was true (for obvious reasons). The English archeologist Sir Arthur Evans believed the story was based on fact, however, and went to Crete to excavate. At Knossos he found the ruins of a structure which he called "The Palace of King Minos" in honor of the myth. We don't know for whom the palace was built. It was constructed, probably piecemeal, around a series of courts, creating an extremely informal, irregular floor plan which may have given rise to the legend of the labyrinth.

Further excavations on the island have unearthed only luxurious houses and palaces -- no fortifications have been found -- suggesting that the Minoans were a peaceable, luxury-loving civilization. They grew

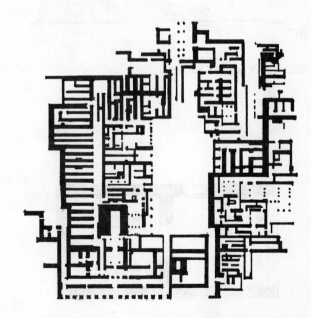

PALACE of KING MINOS

rich through trade and were depicted as traders in Egyptian tomb paintings. Rooms were decorated with paintings on plaster (frescoes) and opened to outside courts and balconies. At least some of their buildings had such "modern" conveniences as running water and flush toilets. The Minoan civilization appears to have been snuffed out by the catastrophic eruption of a volcano, an event which some scholars think generated the myth of Atlantis.

MYCENEAN ARCHITECTURE

The bronze-age culture on the Greek mainland is called Mycenean, named after its capital city of Mycenae. Although influenced by the nearby Minoans, the Myceneans were a stark contrast: warlike, they left many fortress cities which have none of the casual luxury of Minoan residences. The walls around the citadel of Mycenae are typical of their massive stone constructions. They are built of immense blocks of stone which ancients thought could only have been put into place by giants, thus the term "Cyclopean Walls". The race of giants called the Cyclops, like other heroes of Greek myth: Hercules, Orestes, Agamemnon, and Perseus were all associated with Mycenae. In fact it was accounts of Mycenae and its inhabitants in Homer's Illiad which inspired the great German archeologist Schliemann to excavate Mycenae.

Unlike the Minoans but like the Egyptians, the Mycenaens built elaborate tombs. Most of these were underground but some, like the "Treasury of Atreus", contained impressive rooms created by corbelling stone to produce a vault.

The most characteristic and impressive unit of residential architecture was the megaron, an oblong hall. Typically, the lateral walls of the megaron were extended to form a porch, with freestanding columns flanking the entrance. In the center of the megaron might be a hearth framed by four or more columns and an opening above it for smoke. Many scholars believe that the megaron was the ancestor of the Greek temple.

TREASURY of ATREUS

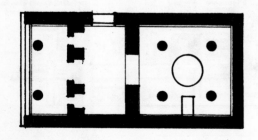

MEGARON

GREEK ARCHITECTURE

HELLENIC ARCHITECTURE

The Mycenean civilization was ended by the "Dorian Invasion". Probably migrating tribes of barbarians from the north conquered the Myceneans. The following four centuries see little produced of artistic value, but at the end of the 8th century occurs one of the greatest turning points in Western History, the emergence of Greek culture.

Greece, a rocky, mountainous land with little arable land and surrounded by the Mediterranean Sea was never a country in antiquity in the sense that Egypt was. Rather it was a collection of small city-states bound by a common language, religion, literature, heroes and love of sports. The ancient Greeks counted their history from the first Olympic games, held in 776 B. C. Politically, these city-states -- Athens and Sparta chief among them -- were constantly fighting mean, treacherous little wars with each other, unified only when threatened by an outside force like Persia or when participating in the Olympics. Yet their achievements in art, architecture, literature, philosophy and mathematics formed the basis of the Western world. The intellectual and artistic achievements of the Greeks belie a total population of free men in ancient Greece less than that of a good-sized American city.

The Greeks were much less interested in inventing new building types and decorations than they were in constantly refining a few. Their architectural vocabulary of plan, form and decoration was limited, and their syntax bounded by strict, impeccably logical rules. Nevertheless, like Mozart writing in the sonata form, the ancient Greek architects achieved buildings of ineffable beauty.

Houses, palaces and tombs interested the Greek architect very little. Fortifications were of only sporadic interest. No expense or effort was spared for civic buildings, however.

The most conspicuous civic structure was the temple. Where geography permitted, it was placed on a hill (an acropolis, literally "high city") above the town and served from afar as symbols of civic pride and accomplishment. The plan of the Greek temple probably derived from the Mycenean megaron unit. (It

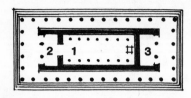

1. noas
2. pronoas
3. opisthodomus

PERIPTERAL TEMPLE

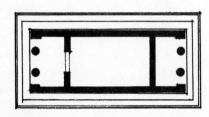

AMPHIPROSTYLE TEMPLE

DORIC ORDER

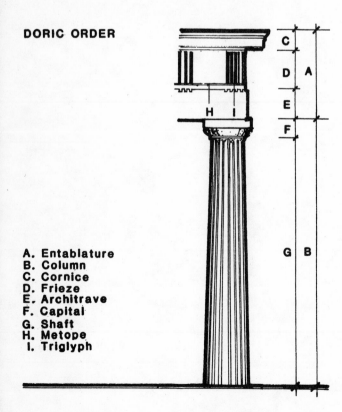

A. Entablature
B. Column
C. Cornice
D. Frieze
E. Architrave
F. Capital
G. Shaft
H. Metope
I. Triglyph

is hardly uncharacteristic for a religious structure to be derived from contemporary residential types; the Temple of Amon-Re at Karnak was an elaboration of the pharaoh's palace, for example.) The megaron became the cella (or naos), the main body of the temple which held a statue of the god to whom the temple was dedicated. The porch of the megaron became the front porch or pronaos. For reasons of symmetry, the Greek architect usually constructed a matching back porch or opisthodomus. The typical Greek temple has a free-standing colonnade on all four sides of the naos. Such a temple is described as peripteral. A few temples have free-standing columns only to the front; they are described as prostyle temples. (A temple with columns both to the front and back is an amphiprostyle temple.)

From very early times, Greek architects accepted that the columns they used and what the columns supported should be designed according to rules as strict as those governing the temple plan. There were three sets of rules, called Orders which obtained in ancient Greece. The Doric Order, the Ionic Order, and the Corinthian Order. These Orders have been used by architects for thousands of years with few modifications. They may still be seen on many buildings in our cites.

The Doric Order is the simplest, the most austere and perhaps the oldest of the three. It is composed of the column (a cylindrical shaft which has no base and a swelling pillow shaped capital at its top) and the entablature (the assembly of parts which the column carries). The entablature is composed of a simple, rectangular beam called the architrave which supports the frieze. The frieze alternates rectangular panels (triglyphs) inscribed with vertical grooves and sculptured rectangular panels called metopes. On top of the frieze is another long, projecting band called the cornice. The larger and more impressive Greek temples almost always used the Doric Order on the exterior.

The Ionic Order, perhaps as old as the Doric but more elegant, varies from it in several important ways. The shaft sits on a base and is thinner in proportion to its height than the Doric. The corners of the Ionic capital end in spiral forms called volutes. The architrave tends to be divided into two or three continuous horizontal bands, and the frieze is one continuous strip, which is sometimes carved. The Ionic Order was used on the interior of many temples and on the exterior of smaller, more elegant ones.

The Corinthian Order was the last of the three to be developed. Except for its capital, it is very similar to the Ionic Order, although its shaft may proportionally be even thinner. The capital is a basket shaped composition of leaves of the acanthus plant, an ornamental weed which grows in the Mediterranean region. This rich capital makes the Corinthian the most elaborate of the Orders. It was rarely used by the ancient Greeks. It was consider too "showy".

Each individual part in an Order (and there are far more than have been listed) had a prescribed mathematical relation to a standard unit of measurement, the MODULE (the radius of the shaft), which was further subdivided into 60 minutes. The shaft in the Doric Order was 11 modules high and the architrave and metope a specified number of minutes, for example. This sort of relationship, which is independent of the absolute size of the Order, is called proportional. It means that if one knows the absolute size of any part of the Order, he can calculate the size of all the other parts. (In one case, an archeologist reconstructed the appearance of an entire temple from one preserved metope. The temple was later excavated. It matched the archeologist's reconstruction perfectly.)

The columns of a Greek temple sat on a platform composed of three continuous steps called the crepidoma (the top step is called the stylobate). On each end, the columns and entablature supported a triangular area (the pediment) which was usually filled with sculptures that had some relation to the god or goddess to whom the temple was dedicated.

The size of a Greek temple and the number of columns in the colonnade varies, but the general layout, appearance, proportions and the rigorous geometry and logic with which the whole is assembled does not. Indeed the Greek temple is, in a sense "artistic geometry". It is a virtual diagram of how a building is constructed using the trabeated system, with the structural function of every part clearly expressed. The posts (columns) and bearing walls (of the cella) are evident at a glance. The column capitals, however decorative, spread out to narrow the effective span between columns. The architrave is a clear depiction of a beam and the frieze a lighter assembly of blocks that mark where the RAFTERS rest on the architrave. The sloping sides of the pediment are the silhouette of the gabled roof. We will call this ap-

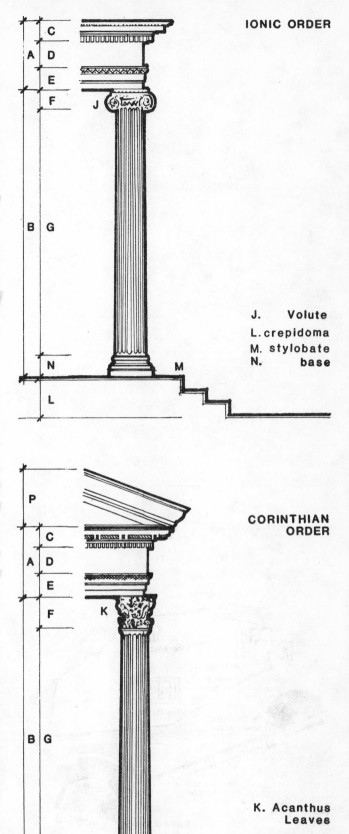

IONIC ORDER

J.   Volute
L. crepidoma
M. stylobate
N.   base

CORINTHIAN ORDER

K. Acanthus Leaves

P. Pediment

proach to architecture, where the reason for being of every structural member of a building is clearly expressed, Rationalist architecture. (The alternate approach, Formalist architecture, will be explained when we discuss Roman architecture.) Some scholars believe that the forms of the Greek temple represent the translation of the primitive wooden temple into stone. This is probably true, but in doing the translation, the Greek architect understood and logically expressed the character and nature of stone construction.

the architecture of Athens

The most famous and refined of the Greek temples, the Parthenon, was built in Athens, the leading intellectual city-state of ancient Greece. It was, however, only the most impressive of a group of temples built on the Athenian Acropolis, high above the city itself. An ancient Mycenean citadel, the Acropolis had been rebuilt several times by the Athenians. The Persians sacked it in 479 B. C., and it was rebuilt in its present form under the brilliant rule of Pericles who introduced radical democracy to Athens.

Pericles' Acropolis was the most splendid and costly group of buildings in Greece. It won the envious admiration of the other city-states (which was what Pericles wanted) but also their enmity since Pericles had embezzled from a mutual defense fund to pay for the buildings.

Individually, the temples on the Acropolis demonstrate the rational geometry beloved of the Greeks. As a group, they are arranged in no perceptible pattern, however. Their placement depended more on the irregular shape of the natural outcropping which forms the Acropolis and the sacred character of certain places where temples had long stood. Nevertheless, the composition which resulted is probably the best-loved grouping of buildings in the world.

There was only one approach to these temples. A path led up from the city to the Propylaea, the entry gate which also housed one of the earliest art museums known. Once through it, the view was dominated by the Parthenon, which many people still consider the most perfect building ever built.

The Parthenon was approached from the west, its rear or opisthodomus end, not the entry facade. This

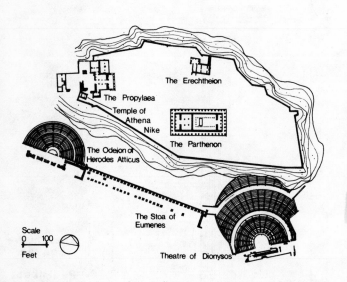

The Erechtheion

The Propylaea

Temple of Athena Nike

The Odeion of Herodes Atticus

The Parthenon

The Stoa of Eumenes

Theatre of Dionysos

Scale
0   100
Feet

THE ACROPOLIS   Athens

orientation would be curious for a modern religious structure, but **the public was not permitted to enter a Greek temple.** The worshipper was permitted to look through the open door of the cella to see the huge, gold and ivory statue of Athena, the eponymous patron goddess of Athens. The Greek temple served as symbolic house for the gods, but it was not more than a **background** for most religious ceremonies. They took place in the open air in front of it.

The sculptor Phidias was originally put in charge of the Parthenon, but two architects, Ictinus and Callicrates are credited with its design. Phidias was later accused of embezzling money intended for the building (probably untrue) and dismissed. Before leaving he executed, with the help of many assistants, three superb groups of sculpture for the Parthenon.

A visitor would first have seen the sculptures in the west pediment, a group of statues showing the contest between Athena and Poseidon, the god of the sea which determined which would be the patron of Athens. Athena won, of course, and her birth is represented in the east pediment. Each metope had a RELIEF sculpture which illustrated battles between the Lapiths and the Centaurs. The Lapiths were mythical Greeks and the centaurs were creatures that were half men, half horse. The Lapiths win. For the ancient Greeks, these reliefs represented the constant battle between civilized man (the Greeks) and barbarians (for the Greeks, barbarian meant anyone who wasn't Greek). The third group of sculptures could only be seen by walking under the colonnade. It was a continuous relief running around the top of the cella wall which depicted the Panathenaic Procession, a great festival which ended in a parade up to the Acropolis.

The sculpture is exquistitely executed. The Parthenon would probably be famous for it alone, but for those that appreciate fine architecture, it is the summit of that art because of the subtle proportions, not only in the Orders but throughout the building, and for the manner in which the architects have countered distortions which are inherent in the way humans see. A perfectly cylindrical column would appear concave or "pinched" in the center, so the Greek architect tapers the column slightly and in the Parthenon makes the shaft bulge slightly. This slight curvature of the shaft is called entasis. As a result the column **looks** cylindrical. The corners of the colonnade would appear weak if they were spaced as far from the

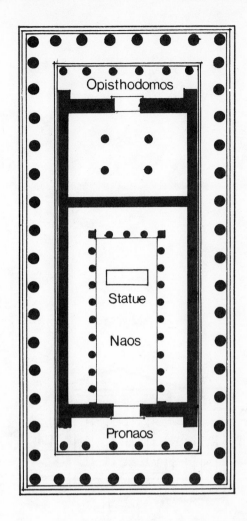

plan   PARTHENON

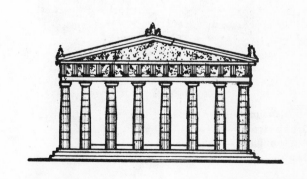

east elevation   PARTHENON

next column as the middle columns are, so Ictinus and Callicrates moved them somewhat closer to the neighboring columns. A long horizontal like the top surface of the stylobate and the bottom of the architrave appears to sag in the middle, so in the Parthenon both are bowed slightly up in the center to balance this perception. All of these optical corrections are subtle. They are not obvious to the average visitor until they are pointed out, but their presence shows the remarkable sensitivity of the architects of the Parthenon. To be sure, reason and geometry govern, but they are softened and made poetic by subjugating them to human feeling.

Two other buildings on the Acropolis demonstrate exceptions to the general rules governing the design of the Greek temple which have been sketched out. The most eccentric temple in Greece is probably the one to the north of the Parthenon called the Erechtheion. It appears to be assembled from parts of three different buildings, designed by three different architects who never talked to each other. Each part is elegantly detailed, but most of the rules of Greek architecture seem to have been broken in the overall composition of the parts. The Erechtheion probably looks as it does because it housed three different and competing cults whose traditionally sacred spots were so close together that their shrines touch. An especially curious, but beautiful, aspect of the building is the substitution of statues of maidens (caryatids) for columns on one of the porches.

The Temple of Athena Nike is as pristine an architectural jewel as the Erechtheion is clumsy. The tiny Nike temple sits on a forward bastion of the Acropolis. It is rectangular in plan like the Parthenon, but is amphiprostyle rather than peripteral and uses the Ionic Order rather than the Doric on the exterior.

At the foot of the Acropolis was the civic center and market area (agora) of ancient Athens. Quotidian civic meetings and political discussions took place in long, colonnaded structures called stoas. The most popular public entertainments in ancient Greece (in all cities, not just Athens) took place in nearby theaters. Plays were originally considered lower-class entertainments in contrast to sports, which were considered upper-class. The typical theater was shaped like the letter "D" and carefully located on a hillside so that the semi-circular seating area (the auditorium) could take advantage of the natural slope of the hill. A circular area called the orchestra at the bot-

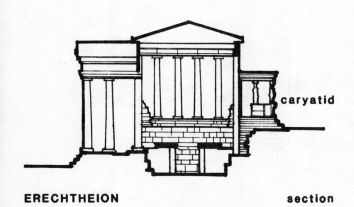

ERECHTHEION   caryatid

ERECHTHEION   section

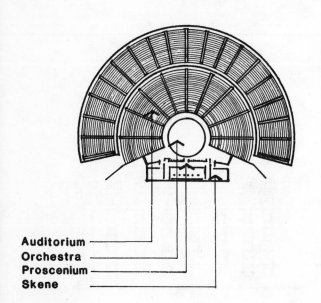

Auditorium
Orchestra
Proscenium
Skene

THEATER   plan

tom of the auditorium provided space for a chorus which commented on the action of the play. The straight side of the "D" was the scene building (or skene) where props were stored and actors waited. The facade of the skene served as a backdrop for the proscenium (proskenion). Because of the tight circle and sharp slope of seats, the acoustics in a Greek theater were excellent. Anyone familiar with modern theater will recognize that all the old Greek words are still used to refer to parts of a theater.

HELLENISTIC ARCHITECTURE

The continued petty squabbling among the Greek city-states destroyed them. In 323 B. C. Greece was conquered by the brilliant young Macedonian warrior Alexander the Great who went on to conquer Egypt and Asia up to the Indus River before he died -- at the age of 32! The empire he conquered was divided up between his generals, the famous Ptolemy taking over Egypt. This empire was called the Hellenistic Empire. Alexander, who had been tutored as a youth by the famous philosopher Aristotle, loved all things Greek. He and the generals who followed him spread Greek culture throughout the territories they conquered.

Hellenistic art and architecture, though based on Greek prototypes which existed before the conquest of Alexander (the Hellenic period) freed itself some-what from the strict Hellenic rules. Hellenistic sculpture is less intellectual, less idealized, thus more realistic than Hellenic. It attempts to show more action and emotion. Hellenistic architecture prefers richer visual effects than Hellenic; it tries to impress by elaboration and grandeur rather than by intellectual subtleties. It prefers variety to refinement of a single type. Hellenistic is especially important historically because it, rather than the "purer" Hellenic architecture, was a major source for the architecture of the Roman Empire.

ETRUSCAN ARCHITECTURE

The Etruscans were another major influence on the Romans. They had been the dominant culture of north-central Italy before the Romans started their conquest of the West. Great traders and engineers in their own right, they were heavily influenced by other cultures, especially the Greeks. It is not always easy to distinguish pottery which was made on mainland Greece from that made by the Etruscans.

The Etruscans were an intensely pragmatic people, performing great feats of practical engineering such as draining swamps for farmland and digging tunnels for water supplies, and they created the sewer system (the Cloaca Maxima) which made it possible to inhabit the low-lying center of what was to become the city of Rome. Their writings are somewhat obscure, but they created the alphabet which is virtually identical to the capital letters used in printing this book.

Their temples look like caricatures when compared to a Greek temple. Built of wood and TERRACOTTA, they have disintegrated. We can reconstruct them from the pieces of terracotta which have survived and clay models which were left in Etruscan tombs, however. The typical Etruscan temple was prostylar and set on a high PODIUM instead a crepidoma. There was a set of steps on the front of the temple only, and few columns to support the simplified entablature.

Much more care was lavished on the Etruscan tomb than other building types. Like the Egyptians, the Etruscans wanted their tombs to be "comfortable". Tombs were largely underground but appear to have mimicked the typical house. Contents of these tombs such as sarcophagi designed to accommodate man and wife together surmounted by terracotta sculptures of the happy couple reinforce the idea that family life was of paramount importance to the Etruscans.

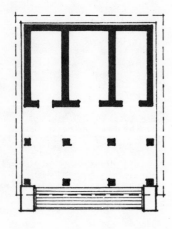

plan

ETRUSCAN TEMPLE   **elevation**

ROMAN ARCHITECTURE

The Romans originally were a local tribal power like the Etruscans, but by 500 B. C. they had began to expand their sphere of influence through intermarriage with other tribes and by conquest. By the beginning of the Christian era they controlled an empire which extended from Scotland in the northwest to North Africa in the south and Asia Minor in the east. The Romans were the dominant power in the West for about 1000 years, but by 500 A. D., the Western Roman Empire had become so weakened for a variety of reasons, including the removal of the capital from Rome to Byzantium (Constantinople), that it succumbed to invading barbarian tribes. The Eastern Roman Empire, however, remained strong and creative until the Middle Ages when first the Christian Crusaders and then the Turkish Moslems snuffed it out.

The West became thoroughly Romanized during the 250 years of peace which followed upon the crowning of Caesar Augustus emperor in 17 A. D. The Roman Empire gradually ceased to be dominated by natives of the Italian peninsula. Indeed, an inhabitant of Roman France or Tunisia felt himself as much a "Roman" as an inhabitant of Rome did. The Romans may have imposed a uniform judicial and governmental structure throughout the Empire, but local religions, customs, and arts were generally respected and assimilated (giving the average citizen a bewildering choice of gods to worship). Their legal, judicial and governmental systems were perhaps the most brilliant innovations of the Romans and so thoroughly accepted and admired in the Empire that they survived its fall and form the basis for most of those societies, including our own, that emerged from the ruins of the Empire.

Roman architecture combined pragmatic planning and engineering skills inherited from the Etruscans with decorative features borrowed from Hellenistic architecture (indeed the architects responsible for decoration of Roman buildings were often Greek) to create an architecture worthy of a great Empire. It was

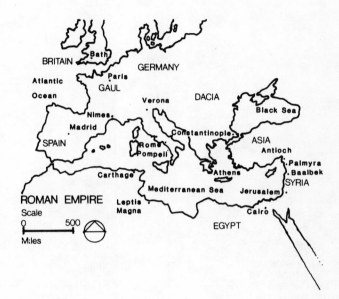

ROMAN EMPIRE
Scale
0   500
Miles

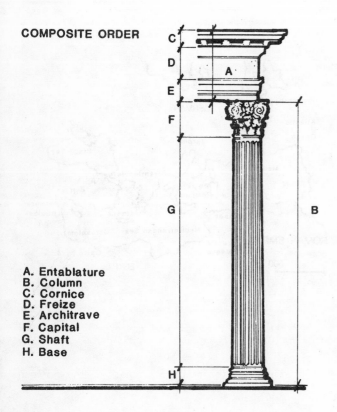

COMPOSITE ORDER

A. Entablature
B. Column
C. Cornice
D. Freize
E. Architrave
F. Capital
G. Shaft
H. Base

architecture meant to overwhelm; to impress by its size, grandeur and opulence rather than by its subtle refinement. Not even the Corinthian Order was sumptuous enough for the Romans, so they combined the volutes of the Ionic capital with the acanthus leaves of the Corinthian capital to create a new, Composite Order (the other details of the Composite Order are similar to the Ionic or Doric).

Interestingly enough, the inherited pragmatism of the Etruscans did not translate into a rationalism like that of the Greeks, where every detail of the building expressed its structural function. Where the Greeks thought of architecture **as** structure, the Romans structured form. They were Formalists; they were interested in the shape and size of buildings and of the shape of the spaces in and around them. They were not particularly concerned with showing what held the building up. The Orders were used primarily as decoration, a sort of symbolic structure or "pseudo-structure" applied on the outside of whatever system was actually used to structure the building.

The most important category of architecture for the Romans was civic architecture: markets, law courts, meeting halls, theaters, public baths and stadiums for sporting events. Most of these were built to hold huge crowds -- Imperial Rome was a city of more than a million inhabitants. The limits of the trabeated system made it inappropriate for such immense structures, and the Romans adapted the arcuated system from the Middle East, where it had been developed. They managed to overcome **its** limitations by developing a new material and new techniques of construction.

The new material was a form of concrete. Concrete is a mixture of cement (a sort of "dehydrated limestone"); a fine aggregate (sand) and a large, coarse aggregate (rocks and bricks). When water is combined with this mixture it first turns into a thick slurry which may be poured into formwork of nearly any shape. A chemical reaction takes place and the slurry solidifies, turning into an artificial stone of great compressive (but little tensile) strength. This "artificial stone" behaves structurally very much like stone masonry. Unless reinforced with some material capable of resisting tension (a technique which was developed much later to create modern reinforced concrete), concrete construction does not drastically reduce the inherent limitations of the trabeabeated system. It does, however, give new life to the arcuated system.

Gradually, the Romans realized the potential of a concrete arcuated system, building not only arches, but also barrel vaults and domes. Since concrete is liquid when it is poured onto centering, no voussoirs are needed; there is none of the painstaking carving of each individually-shaped stone. Unskilled slaves may be used for the undemanding work of mixing and pouring concrete. Buildings of immense size which can be built quickly and relatively economically are possible with this method.

Roman concrete construction had two serious drawbacks. First of all, it took as much as five years to achieve its great strength (versus about a month for modern concrete); in principle, the formwork must be left in place for most of this period. Secondly, when the formwork is removed, the bare surface of the concrete (not very attractive in the case of Roman concrete) was exposed, requiring another material to be applied to decorate it. The Romans overcame both drawbacks by making the formwork a decorative, integral part of the finished concrete. In building a wall, for example, they laid up two outer surfaces of specially shaped brick or stone with points facing into the void between them. When concrete was poured into this cavity, it was held in place by these surfaces which then acted as permanent formwork and could serve as the finished surface of the wall.

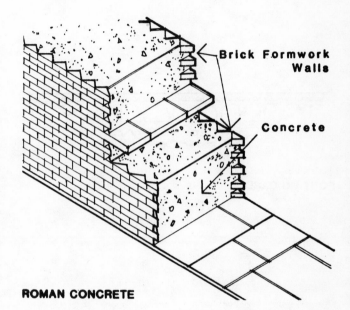

ROMAN CONCRETE

Brick Formwork Walls

Concrete

EXAMPLES OF ROMAN ARCHITECTURE

Vitruvius, active from 46-30 B. C, wrote about the principles of Roman architecture in his book De Architectura (Ten Books of Architecture). It was the only book on architecture to survive from antiquity and was one of the major architectural text books until recent times as well as our best source on the theory of ancient architecture (although Vitruvius must be taken with a grain of salt). As we have mentioned above, our criteria of Firmness, Commodity and Delight are borrowed from Vitruvius. He wrote during the period of history when Rome was a Republic and before concrete was used extensively.

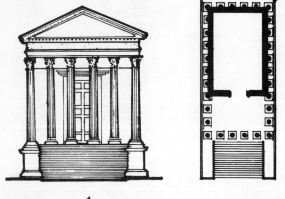

MAISON CARÉE

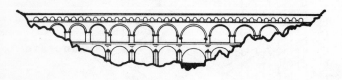

PONT DU GARD

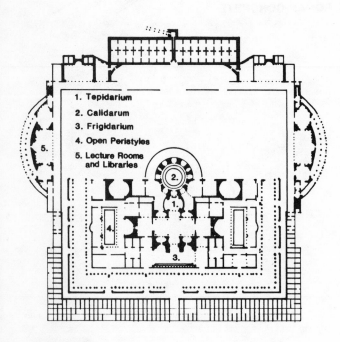

1. Tepidarium
2. Calidarum
3. Frigidarium
4. Open Peristyles
5. Lecture Rooms and Libraries

ROMAN BATH

Republican architecture was still relatively conservative. Though built at the beginning of the Empire, the Maison Carée at Nimes, France, is typical of the Republican Roman temple. It generally takes over the forms of the Greek-inspired Etruscan temple. Prostylar, with a distinct front and back, it gives a first impression of being peripteral. Only the columns of the porch are freestanding, however; those along the cella are engaged columns (half-columns applied to the face of a wall). The Roman temple is pseudo-peripteral. Like the Etruscan, the Roman temple sits on a high podium, and there are stairs only on the entry facade. Unlike the Greek temples on their acropoli, Roman temples were most commonly included in the heart of the forum or market areas of the Roman city.

The Roman temple, like most Republican architecture, was trabeated; but the arch was also introduced relatively early. It was considered so important and characteristic a form that arches were constructed as free-standing monuments (the triumphal arch) to commemorate victories and to serve as the entry gates to cities.

The Pont du Gard in France, also a Republican structure, is a good example of utilitarian Roman architecture. It uses the arch, in this case an arcade, to span the river Gard. Quite a handsome and impressive structure for a mere AQUEDUCT which carried water to Nimes, the Pont du Gard represents the Roman preoccupation with supplying superior water in large quantities to their cities for drinking and bathing.

The bath was among the largest and most impressive types of civic structures in Rome. The great Imperial Roman Baths of Caracella, for example, covered some 50 acres. The sheer size of such public baths would not have been possible without the development of concrete construction. Baths were social meeting places as well as centers for hygiene and comprised a complex of rooms, each suited to a specific hygienic, social or educational function. The typical bath included a frigidarium (cold room), a tepidarium (warm room), a caldarium (hot room), the natatorium (swimming pool), dressing rooms and "saunas", and a palestra (exercise fields) as well as libraries and meeting rooms. The Roman architect demonstrates his characteristic skill at planning in organizing all these varied sizes and shapes of rooms into an impressive but unified whole. Rooms and spaces are arranged along AXES and cross-axes to create a complex, symmetrical plan and long vistas through the variety of functional spaces.

The Romans built various other entertainment structures, especially theaters and amphitheaters (literally "two-theaters") the most famous of which was the Flavian Amphitheater in Rome (nicknamed the "Colosseum"). It was 159 feet high and seated about 55,000 spectators. Instead of using Orders which extended the entire height to decorate the exterior, the architects divided the facade into four stories and superimposed Orders. They used Doric engaged columns on the ground floor, Ionic on the second and Corinthian on the third. For the top story they changed to engaged Corinthian PILASTERS. The Colosseum is still a model example of how to handle huge crowds in a public place. Historians estimate that the entire audience could leave it in about 5 minutes. Architects were still experimenting with the potential of concrete when building the Colosseum. It makes extensive use of concrete in the vaulting which holds up the seating, but most of the rest of the amphitheater was built of stone. The lessons learned from using concrete were picked and expanded on by other architects, however.

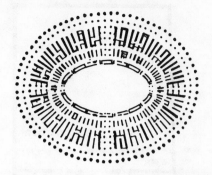

ROMAN AMPHITHEATRE

Probably the most spectacular use of concrete, probably the single most spectacular building which the ancient Romans have left us is "the Pantheon, the most celebrated building in the whole world." It was was built by the Emperor Hadrian who may have been its architect (118-128 B. C.) and was preserved almost intact because it was turned into a Christian church. Its circular plan, its immense dome and the details of its decoration probably refer to the universe as the Romans thought of it and to the fact that it was intended to honor all the gods. The circular form permits emphasis to be spread equally around the interior, and a dome was even then an architectural symbol for the sky/heaven; the dome has 28 ribs (the days of the month) and the oculus (an "eye" or hole in the center of the dome, which is the only source of natural light) may represent the sun. Even today, one is hardly prepared for the impact of the powerful domed space -- 142 feet in diameter and 142 feet high. In antiquity, the contrast between the typical, pedimented porch and the interior was even greater. The ground level was lower than it presently is, and an entry court helped screen the the dome and heighten the surprise of the interior. The entire structure is built of concrete, with 20 foot thick walls to contain the thrusts of the great dome. Hadrian and his assistants very cleverly made the

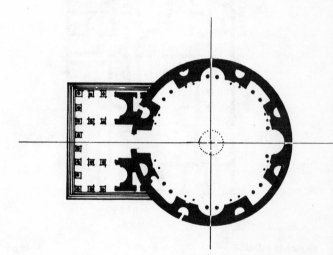

plan   **THE PANTHEON**

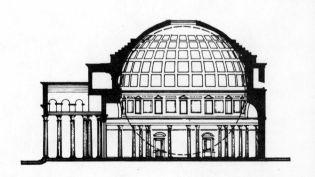

section   **THE PANTHEON**

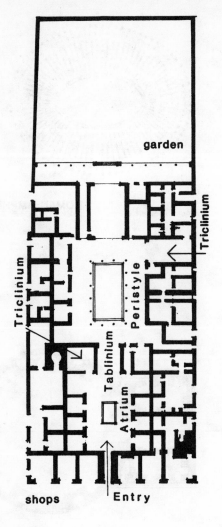

ROMAN HOUSE   **domus**

dome both visually and physically lighter by hollowing out squares (coffers) on its inner surface. The Pantheon may well be the single most influential building ever built.

At the opposite end of the scale from the baths and amphitheaters were houses and apartments. Wealthier Romans lived in low houses which had rooms arranged around one or more interior courtyards or atria (singular, atrium) and a garden at the back of the house. The atrium house was inward focusing (there were few if any windows on the exterior of the house) and had developed from traditional domestic architecture of the Mediterranean area. Originally the room on the opposite side of the atrium from the entry was the tablinum, the main reception room of the house. Next to it was the triclinium or dining room. As a Roman family became wealthier, the house was extended into the garden around a peristyle, a courtyard which ringed with columns. The peristyle was as light and airy as the atrium was dark and cavernous. Summer triclinia, reception rooms and bedrooms opened off the peristyle. This type of expanded Roman house was especially typical of country, resort cities like Pompeii and Herculaneum. The latter two cities preserve many examples of the Roman house since they were covered by the eruption of Mt. Vesuvius in 79 A. D. and only uncovered in the last two centuries.

Poorer citizens, especially in big cities like Rome, lived in multi-storied apartment buildings called insulae (singular, "insula"). These were built of brick and concrete and often reached as high as seven stories. A single floor might have several apartments arranged around courtyards which penetrated the top several floors of the insula. The ground floor was usually given over to shops and light industry. The rebuilding of Rome after the Renaissance destroyed the insulae, but the working-class port city of Rome, Ostia, preserves a number of them.

Wealthy city dwellers also had country homes or villas which resembled large, spread-out city homes but with more rooms open to the countryside. Since the fortunes of many Roman families depended on extensive agricultural holdings, these villa-estates were often working farms as well as country retreats.

EARLY CHRISTIAN ARCHITECTURE

In 313 A. D., the Roman Emperor Constantine was converted to Christianity. His Edict of Milan made it an official state religion, and because the Emperor himself was a Christian, Christianity rapidly became the dominant religion of the Roman Empire. Until this time, Christians had been sporadically persecuted. They had met in houses, converted for the purpose, both because that made them less conspicuous and because most of the early Christians were poor. Thus until the time of Constantine, there was no special type of architecture for the church.

With the vastly increased popularity of Christianity came the need to accommodate large congregations. Constantine's architects adapted the basilica for the new churches. The basilica, a large, longitudinal, structure with a high central space (nave) and lower spaces flanking it to either side (aisles), had been a utilitarian civic building used by the Romans for many purposes: law courts, markets, etc. It was perfectly adapted to the new religion and in addition, as a secular building type, had no connotations with the pagan religions. The nave accommodated Christian processions and the raised, curved area at the end of the nave, which had been the seat of the magistrate in the law court, could be adapted for the altar and the chair of the bishop. In these early churches, it was considered desirable that a Christian upon entering would come from the east (symbolizing the rising sun, the birth of Christ, baptism) and face west (the altar, the table of the Last Supper, and the setting sun). Since one faced west (the occident) upon entering, we say these churches were occidented".

Constantinian basilicas such as Old St. Peter's Basilica or St Paul's Outside the Walls were vast structures. The roofs, instead of being concrete vaults were usually wooden trusses. The interiors were lit by clerestory windows placed in the area of wall between the roof of the outer aisle (or aisles) and the roof of the nave. Wall surfaces were covered with frescoes or mosaics, decorations made by embedding small cubes of glass or precious stones in plaster).

Another type of church or monument called a martyrium was developed to mark holy sites like the burial

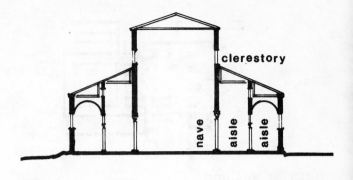

section

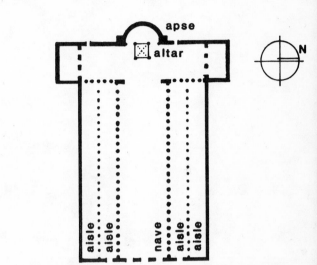

plan

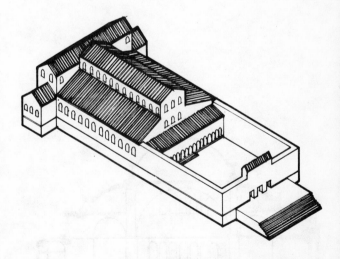

isometric   OLD ST. PETER'S

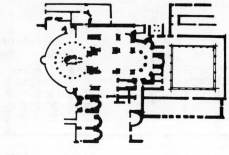

HOLY SEPULCHRE

places of holy people or places where Christians had been martyred. A martyrium is usually <u>centralized</u>, that is, it is symmetrical about more than one axis (circles, octagons, etc.) so that it focuses on a central point -- the point to be remembered. A martyrium was built very early in the Christian era to mark the spot in Jerusalem where, according to Christian belief, Christ was entombed <u>The Church of the Holy Sepulchre</u>.

BYZANTINE ARCHITECTURE

By 330 A. D. the eastern part of the Roman Empire had become much wealthier and more sophisticated than the west, and Constantine moved the capital of the Empire from Rome to <u>Byzantium</u>, which was renamed <u>Constantinople</u> (modern Istanbul). With the government gone, the city of Rome lost its reason for being and went into a decline which was exacerbated by moving what government had remained in Rome to Ravenna, a small city on the east coast of Italy which had better sea connections to Constantinople. The decline of the government in the West was accompanied by a decline in the army. The West was splintered by waves of <u>barbarian invasions</u>. In 476 A. D. a barbarian king took over power in Ravenna. The Western Roman Empire had technically fallen, although Roman governmental structures continued on a local level and people continued to speak Latin in most of Europe for the next couple centuries.

The Eastern Empire continued to flourish in Constantinople. Under the Emperor <u>Justinian</u> and his brilliant wife <u>Theodora</u> some of the territory lost to the barbarians was recouped and a new high point of Roman culture, the <u>Byzantine</u> culture was achieved. The major monument of this period was the church of <u>Hagia Sophia</u> (Holy Wisdom) in Constantinople. Justinian and Theodora commissioned it -- the equal to the Parthenon or Pantheon in architectural significance -- from <u>Anthemios of Tralles</u> and <u>Isidorus of Miletus</u>. Anthemios was the most famous architect of his day and also one of the most expert mathematicians. He was told by Justinian to spare no expense to make a building worthy of the "new Golden Age". Ancient records say that 10,000 workers were employed on the building.

HAGIA SOPHIA   **section**

Both the plan and method of structuring Hagia Sophia were innovative. The plan combines qualities of the basilica with those of the centralized plan: there is a nave and two side aisles like a basilica, but the central bay of the nave is a great square which is crowned by a dome. Two half-domes of the same diameter are used on the east and west to buttress the great dome, and these in turn are buttressed by smaller semi-domes; to the north and south, the central dome is buttressed by vaults over the side aisles. The thrusts of domes and vaults are carried down to four main PIERS at the corners of the square nave under the dome and to smaller piers at the outer walls. Anthemios' brilliance as a geometer shows up in his solution for making the visual and structural transition from the circle, which was the base of the dome, to the four points, which were the tops of the corner piers. He uses spherical triangles called pen- dentives; the bases of the pendentives touch to form a circle, their apexes touch the tops of the piers. The spatial effects in the completed building are impressive. If one looks straight ahead upon entering, the directional character of the plan at ground level leads ones eyes (or a procession) to the altar at the far end of the nave; but if one looks up, he has the sense that all the subspaces of the church build up to the great dome in the center.

The system of structuring Hagia Sophia was a stroke of brilliance, but the methods used to construct it lead to a disaster. Because Justinian wanted his church built quickly, Isidorus and Anthemios used brick with very thick mortar joints to construct the great piers and domes. The mortar, like Roman con- crete, set very slowly, however, and the thrusts of the dome pushed the piers apart. The great dome fell within a few years of construction and had to be rebuilt. By this time the mortar had set, and the church has since withstood time and earthquake. Hagia Sophia was made into a mosque after the Mos- lems conquered the Byzantine Empire in 1453. The Turkish government has recently turned it into a museum.

Hagia Sophia is the most spectacular example of Byz- antine architecture, but there are many other splen- did examples, several of which are in Ravenna.

Some churches there like San Vitale show the same sort of spatial complexity as Hagia Sophia, but others such as San Apollinare are modifications of the Early Christian basilican plan. All (including Hagia Sophia

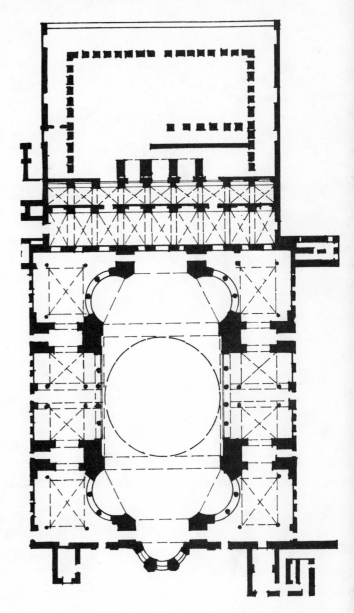

plan   **HAGIA SOPHIA**

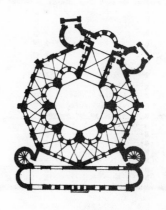

plan   **SAN VITALE**

itself) are made glorious by the rich mosaic decorations, so characteristic of Byzantine architecture, which cover virtually every wall surface.

MOSLEM (ISLAMIC) ARCHITECTURE

The Moslem religion (Islam) spread rapidly over the Near East, North Africa and into Spain after the Prophet Mohammed's death in 632 A. D., almost exactly a century after Hagia Sophia was built. The Islamic liturgy is much simpler than Christianity's, so a wide variety of structures may be adapted to become a mosque, the major religious structure of Islam. A mosque must have the following features, however: a fountain for washing before entering the sanctuary; a space large enough for worshippers to kneel and pray; a prayer niche (mihrab) indicating qibla, the direction of Mecca (the holiest city of Islam, a city in Saudi Arabia); a mimbar, a pulpit from which the sermon is preached on Fridays; and a tower on the exterior of the mosque (minaret) from which a muezzin sings the call to prayer.

As with many other religions, the Mohammedans used the house as the basis for their earliest sanctuaries. In this case it was Mohammed's courtyard-house in Medina. Because the architectural requirements of a mosque are simple, Moslems often adapted local building traditions for their mosques. The simple requirements also made it easy to continually expand mosques to accommodate growing populations. A superb example is the Great Mosque of Cordoba (Spain) which was begun in 785 A. D. but expanded over the next 200 years. (It was somewhat brutally transformed into a Catholic church at a later date, but much of the character of the interior, with its seemingly endless rows of columns, remains.) One law of Islam that is reflected in the decoration of all Moslem structures is the prohibition of images of man and animals. Thus the beautiful Arabic calligraphy is used as a basis for decorations (usually quotations from the Koran, the holy book of Islam).

Much Islamic architecture is religious, but there are also Moslem houses and palaces of great beauty and refinement. The Alhambra in Granada, Spain, is a masterpiece of domestic architecture. It is organized around courtyards, and water is lead through every room and court to create tranquil micro-climates.

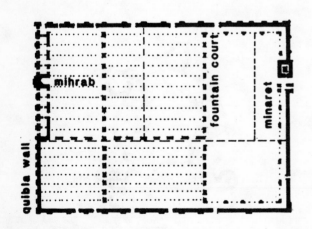

GREAT MOSQUE   CORDOBA

ARCHITECTURE OF THE DARK AND MIDDLE AGES

MAP OF THE PILGRIMAGE ROUTES

In the 12th and 13th centuries, very "international" even by modern standards, well-defined Pilgrimage Routes were established in Europe which ended in Santiago da Compostella in northwestern Spain where, the pilgrims believed, the body of the Apostle James was buried. The purpose of these pilgrimages was to visit holy sites of Christendom and thereby gain favor with God. The extensive flow of pilgrims, encouraged especially by the powerful abbey of Cluny in France, also stimulated the economy, encourage the building of great churches and hostels along the routes and diffused information rapidly throughout Europe.

THE DARK AGES

The waves of migrations and invasions by tribes from Central Europe (Ostrogoths, Visigoths and Vandals) gradually reduced the ordered Western Roman Empire into anarchy. Centralized government broke down under the onslaughts of these uneducated, uncivilized, nomadic, peoples who had been forced into the Empire by pressures from the Huns. The first waves of migrations were assimilated by the Roman citizens, but as more and more migrants arrived it must be said that they assimilated the Roman culture, which became more and more diluted by northern, barbaric traditions. Trade gradually diminished to nothing; the moneyed economy of the Romans was replaced by a barter economy; the Roman army was replaced by unruly bands of local armed men; Roman magistrates were replaced by war lords. In this atmosphere, cities could no longer exist, and the population, radically decreased, dispersed into the countryside. Literacy existed only within the Church.

Because the barbarian tribes were nomads, their building traditions were limited. Their art consisted of producing relatively small, portable objects. As a result, we find very little impressive architecture from the "Dark Ages", the years roughly between 700 and 1000 A. D. Some exquisite jewelry and manuscripts survive from this period, however. One such manuscript, the Book of Kells, a marvelously illustrated book of the Gospels, is one of the most beautiful books ever produced. Such manuscripts and jewelry from this time show the artistic preferences of the northern barbarians: a love of the geometric, of nature and of linear patterns. The Dark Ages were by no means pitch black.

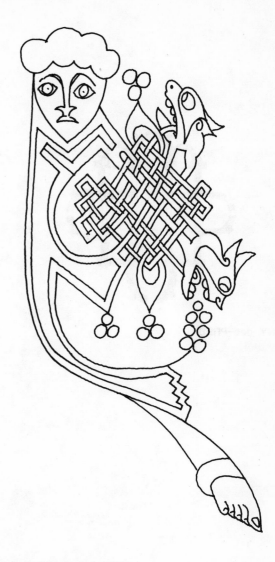

THE BOOK OF KELLS

CAROLINGIAN ARCHITECTURE

Towards the end of the 8th century, a soldier from northern Europe named Charlemagne (or Carolus Magnus in Latin, thus the name Carolingian) reconquered much of the former Western Roman Empire. His goal was to create a new, Christianized, Roman Empire -- a Holy Roman Empire -- and as a first step he went to Rome and forced the Pope to crown him Holy Roman Emperor on Christmas Day, 800 A. D.

The title was passed down to modern times. Charlemagne gathered around him the brightest artists, scholars and architects from the territories he had conquered and bade them study the remains of Roman culture and reproduce what they could. The results were remarkable, although the centuries of neglect of Roman traditions and the influence of northern barbaric traditions are obvious to us when we look today at the works produced in his court. At his palace in Aachen, Germany (Aix-la-Chapelle) he had his architects "reconstruct" a facsimile of San Vitale in Ravenna as his palace chapel. His bishop constructed a private chapel at Germigny-des-Prés in France. This chapel, a beautiful but small building, is more a reflection of what was "new" at the time than a reconstruction of anything Roman. Influences of contemporary Spanish and Byzantine architecture are evident in its GREEK CROSS plan (inscribed in a square) and the Byzantine-inspired mosaics which decorate the interior.

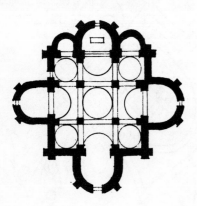

GERMINY-des-PRES

MEDIEVAL ARCHITECTURE

The unified Carolingian Empire did not outlast Charlemagne by much. Traditions of inheritance caused Charlemagne's Empire to be divided between his three sons, and a new series of barbarian invasions by the Vikings (tribes from Scandinavia) reduced society once more to relative anarchy. A feudal system evolved as a form of government. Families in a small area would recognize one of their members as a leader; he would assure a strong point (a fortress) for their protection and organize warriors (knights) for mutual defense. In return, the peasants recognized the lord as owning all land and having the right to expect them to supply him with food and various other services. He, in turn, would owe certain responsibilities (especially military service along with his knights) to a more powerful lord in return for that lord's protection. In principle, all lords in a large region owed similar responsibilities to a king. In practice, however, the lords would fight with each other -- and even the king -- for more territory and for prestige. The times were very unsettled. The only islands of stability and learning (virtually all the lords and knights were illiterate) in this period were the monasteries.

The monastery was a community of men who had left active society and renounced marriage, wealth and career for a life dedicated to the Church. Monasteries began in Egypt fairly early in the Christian era and gradually spread to Italy. There, St. Benedict wrote down the Rule, actually a set of rules, which prescribed every detail of a monk's life. The major duties of a monk were to pray and sing praises to God and to copy the Bible and other religious writings. Consequently it was important that the monks could read and write. They kept learning alive during the Dark and Early Middle Ages. Other than the lords who commissioned castles (mostly built of wood until Gothic times), the monasteries were the major patrons of architecture during these periods.

The architecture of the monastery directly reflected the activities that went on in them. They were isolated in the countryside and internalized around a central courtyard like the Roman villa (after which the first ones were, to a degree, patterned), closed against the outside world for both symbolic reasons and for protection against barbarian attacks. This courtyard, the heart of activity in a monastery is called a cloister. Around the cloister were arranged: the church for devotions; the dormitory (a communal space in most monasteries); the refectory (dining hall); the scriptorium, a combination library and workroom where the monks copied or wrote and illustrated books on pieces of animal skin; the chapter house, where organizational meetings were held and chapters of the Rule were read; and other service buildings.

By about 1000 A. D., the Vikings had mostly been assimilated into Europe (many of them, "Norsemen", settled in northwestern France, which became known as Normandy). The feudal system had begun to offer some political stability, and the monasteries had become extremely wealthy from the inheritances left them over generations. In this atmosphere trade, and with it a moneyed economy, began to revive. Political stability and trade generated towns and cities. A new period of vital creativity was stimulated. This period, the Middle Ages, is customarily divided into two parts: the Romanesque period and the Gothic period. Though the two in fact run into each other without clear separation, each period can be distinguished, especially by its architecture.

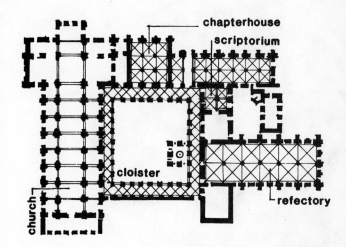

MONASTERY AT FONTENAY

ROMANESQUE ARCHITECTURE

During the later Romanesque period, large buildings like churches were built by professional masons, but during the early Romanesque, the monasteries not only commissioned most of the significant architecture, they also supplied the craftsmen who built it, usually monks or local craftsmen associated with the monastery. These people were not trained in the art of building; consequently, early Romanesque churches are unsophisticated (but remarkably appealing, much like a folk-song): small and homely; structurally conservative; cave-like and decorated with beasts and patterns that suggest the nature worship of their barbaric ancestors was still strong. Since these builders were not skilled craftsmen, cut stone was used only where absolutely necessary (in arches and the outer facings of walls). Otherwise, these buildings were made of stacked RUBBLE.

As monasteries grew wealthier during the course of the 11th century, they came to control vast tracts of land and became great secular as well as religious forces. In fact the monastery of Cluny in France controlled not only its own estates but over 1500 monasteries from Poland to England. Given the nature of the feudal system, Cluny was the most powerful political entity in Europe. Indeed the mother church was only a few feet shorter than St. Peter's in Rome, the largest building in Christendom.

With Cluny leading the way, monasteries commissioned ever larger structures and encouraged pilgrims (religious tourists, in the context of the Middle Ages) to visit them by collecting and exhibiting relics (parts of the bodies of saints or furnishings connected with them) as attractions. The pilgrims donated money to the monasteries and made them even wealthier. Even grander churches were constructed which attracted more pilgrims.

Pilgrimages became a social phenomenon in and of themselves and utterly changed medieval society. The ultimate goal of the medieval pilgrim was Jerusalem; if he could not afford to go there, he tried to visit Rome; and if Rome was beyond his means, Santiago

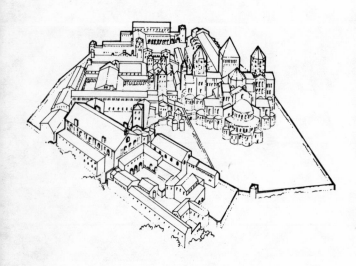

CLUNY

da Compostella in northern Spain was his goal. The poorest of pilgrims searched out some other church with famous relics. (Chaucer's Canterbury Tales recounts the experiences of pilgrims on their way to Canterbury.)

Besides their enormous impact on the medieval economy, pilgrimages also served to rapidly diffuse information across Europe and the Middle East. The latest news, scholarship and technical innovations were exchanged among travelers on the pilgrimage routes.

The most important side effect of the pilgrimages was the Crusades, military expeditions of knights from across Europe sent to capture the Holy Land from the Moslems and make it safe for Christians to visit. (Here, too, Cluny was the driving force.) The military campaign was only partly successful, but Crusader contacts with Islamic culture and with the Byzantine Empire were of inestimable value in stimulating the awakening intellect of Europe. Both of the middle eastern civilizations had guarded the science, literature and philosophy of antiquity which was lost during the Dark Ages in Europe. The Moslems also had a superior building technology which the Crusaders brought back to Europe and introduced into the new pilgrimage churches and castles.

THE ROMANESQUE PILGRIMAGE CHURCH

The architecture of the pilgrimages at their height (the first half of the 12th century) was a synthesis of the northern wood tradition; early Romanesque architecture, which revived some Roman forms and techniques (the arcuated system and masonry construction); and forms, building techniques and decorative details borrowed from contacts with the Byzantines and Moslems. It was the first truly **European** architecture.

The Pilgrimage church had to accommodate both processions of great crowds who wanted to visit the relics in the churches and the need for each monk in the monasteries who built and maintained these churches to say mass every day. The plan which evolved to meet these requirements was basilican in the form of a **LATIN CROSS:** a long nave was flanked on each side by one or two aisles and intersected by short arms, transverse naves called transepts. The rectangular area (or crossing) where nave

SAINTE-FOY   **CONQUES**

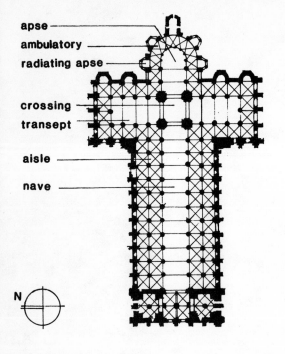

apse
ambulatory
radiating apse

crossing
transept

aisle

nave

N

ST. SERNIN   **plan**

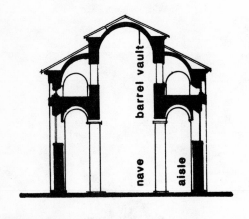

barrel vault

nave   aisle

ROMANESQUE CHURCH   **section**

and transepts intersected formed a focus in front of the main altar, which was located in the semi-circular apse that terminated the main nave. To accommodate monks and relics, a number of smaller apse-like chapels (apsidioles) were built along the transepts and the apse. The side aisles were continued around the apse between apsidioles and the altar, forming an orderly path for the pilgrims, an ambulatory, so that they could visit the relics (or the monks could say their own masses) at the same time that services were being held in the main part of the church. The radial pattern of the apsidioles around the apse (radiating apse), though characteristic of the pilgrimage church, was used for centuries, even in churches that had little connection with pilgrimages. Typical examples of the great pilgrimage church are Sainte-Foy at Conques, France and St. Sernin in Toulouse (also in France, the wealthiest country in Europe during the Middle Ages). Cluny, the largest of the pilgrimage churches, was demolished for building stone after the French Revolution.

Most of these churches were oriented. That is, a pilgrim would have faced **east** -- Jerusalem -- upon entering. (You will remember that the Early Christian church was occidented). Since the setting sun lit up the entry facade, it was often symbolically ornamented with sculpture representing the Last Judgement and Resurrection. Such sculptures at the entrances, those on column capitals, and the frescoes inside the church were more than mere attempts to beautify it, however. They were integral parts of the architecture since almost no one outside of the monasteries could read during the Middle Ages and the Bible was forbidden to lay people. The churches, then, became "books in stone" to educate people.

GOTHIC ARCHITECTURE

The Crusades and pilgrimages, with the accompanying increase in trade, had made European society truly international by the mid 12th century. Although society was still agriculturally based, capitalist enterprise was increasingly important, and cities which owed their existence to international trade prospered and competed with each other. The great churches and city halls which they built became symbols of each city's wealth and pride. Schools attached to the cathedrals began to take the place of the monasteries in educating the public. As literacy became more and more necessary in the new capitalistic society, these cathedral schools became independent entities: the university.

The new wealth and power of the cities and the new levels of learning are clearly evident in the great churches of the period. (Although these large churches are often indiscriminately called cathedrals, the term really only applies to a church headed by a bishop). They were not built by local craftsmen and amateurs as were the early Romanesque churches, but by highly trained and organized professionals who travelled from city to city and country to country. The era of the professional architect and the guild (an ancestor of the modern trade union) had arrived. Both architect and construction worker went through a rigorous training process before they were allowed to become members of a lodge, master-masons. The medieval architect was usually a literate, highly re- spected member of society who may have risen from a mere stone-cutter to a sculptor to master-mason by his ability.

The city-client demanded the most technologically advanced, elaborate and most impressive structure it thought it could afford. ("Let us," said the canons who commissioned Seville Cathedral, "build such and so great a church that those who see it finished will think us mad.") The architects responded by concen- trating more and more of the weight and thrusts of the buildings on smaller and smaller supports creating mere skeletons of stone with glass walls filling the areas between columns. The towns and cities compet- ed to build ever taller buildings. This competition ended with Beauvais Cathedral which is 157 feet high on the interior, as tall as a 15 story skyscraper.

The concentration of loads and thrusts onto columns (with the consequent reduction of walls from bearing structures to mere curtain walls which kept out rain and wind) had begun with the largest of the pilgri- mage churches. The semi-circular BARREL VAULT, even thickened at the columns by bands to concen- trate thrusts, still exerted enormous outward thrusts on the walls. Typically, the vaults over the side aisles were used to counteract these thrusts, but sup- ports and walls had to remain thick and windows small and on outer walls making the interior of these churches fairly dark and somber. At the abbey church of St. Denis north of Paris, several structural innova- tions combined to eliminate most of the problems that frustrated the Romanesque architect in his search for lighter interiors and taller naves.

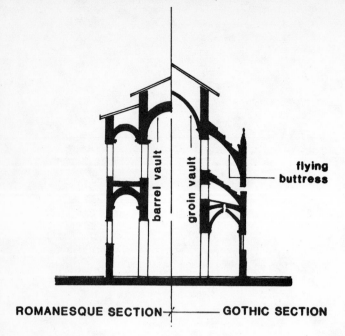

barrel vault | groin vault

flying buttress

ROMANESQUE SECTION ━ GOTHIC SECTION

THE GOTHIC CHURCH

The abbey church of St. Denis is usually considered to be the first <u>Gothic</u> structure. The <u>Abbot Suger</u>, second most powerful man in France and a gentleman of remarkable character, was largely responsible for the innovations. He wanted more light into his old Romanesque church, partly for theological reasons.

The first of the innovations which made Gothic architecture possible was the <u>pointed arch</u>. It directs the thrusts of the vaulting and roof more nearly vertically on the columns than the semi-circular arch. The columns are thus placed more nearly in pure compression; they may therefore be made thinner than Romanesque columns since they don't have to resist as much diagonal thrust. The second innovation was the replacement of the barrel vault by a series of intersecting cross-vaults (<u>groin vaults</u>) which had <u>ribs</u> at the edges where the vaults intersected. Thin <u>panels</u> could then span between the ribs, making the vaulting weigh much less and allowing a further reduction in the size of the columns supporting the vaulting. This <u>rib-and-panel vaulting</u> had the added advantage of being able to cover a structural BAY of any size and shape, whereas intersecting barrel vaults can only cover square bays (if the heights of the the two vaults are to be the same). With these innovations, Suger could install <u>stained glass windows</u> in the outer walls between the columns letting colored light directly into the interior.

A further innovation was introduced in the cathedral of <u>Notre Dame</u> in Paris: the <u>flying buttress</u>. The flying buttress is a sort of arched bridge which carries the diagonal component of thrusts from the vaulting to freestanding towers away from the walls of the church. The columns are now almost purely in compression and can be very thin indeed. (The flying buttresses further make this thinness possible by bracing them and keeping them from buckling.) The Gothic church becomes, as a result, very light inside, for the walls are, to a great degree, glass and the removal of buttress away from the walls permits the sun to shine almost directly on the windows.

With the emphasis on tall, thin columns and windows and soaring vertical spaces, the Gothic architect appreciated the possibility of tying each element of his building into the next larger so that his churches

NAVE ELEVATION   **interior**

build from smallest detail to complete structure in one continuous, unified, dramatic sweep. A High Gothic church stands in extreme contrast, therefore, to a Romanesque church where each part is treated as an individual element or unit **juxtaposed** to the next one. Where a characteristic Romanesque church may be seen as a composition of discrete blocks, the Gothic cathedral is an organic entity where no single part is any more significant than a single leaf or a single branch on a tree.

Sculpture remained an important part of the decoration of the Gothic church, but the frescoes of the Romanesque church were translated into paintings in colored glass. All decoration was more completely integrated into the Gothic building than during the Romanesque period, as one might expect, but it served the same didactic purposes.

These sculptures and stained glass could serve not only to explain religious ideas and stories to the worshippers, they also could argue for the importance of the donors who paid for them, as propaganda against church heresies or, as at Chartres Cathedral, to explain the significance of the cathedral school and its humanist curriculum. The curriculum was based on the Seven Liberal Arts, which still serve as the core of many university curricula. The Seven Liberal Arts were divided into the Trivium (grammar, dialectic and rhetoric) and the Quadrivium (arithmetic, music, geometry and astronomy). This humanism, based on the study of ancient Greek and Roman literature and philosophy, led to a complete reassessment of the relationship between man and God and between man and animal. Ultimately humanism led to a complete reordering of society and its values.

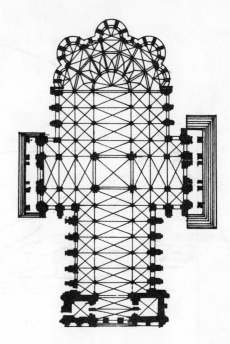

plan   **CHARTRES CATHEDRAL**

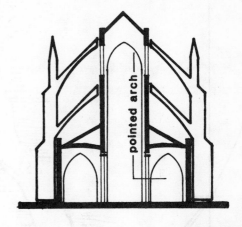

section   **GOTHIC CHURCH**

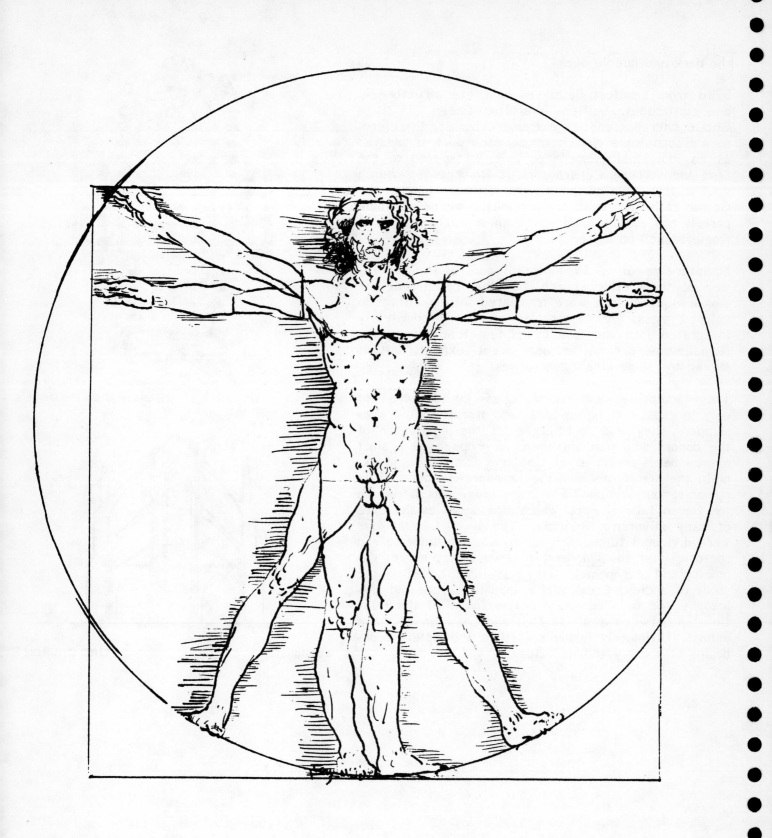

RENAISSANCE AND BAROQUE ARCHITECTURE

VITRUVIAN MAN

When Vitruvius' Ten Books on Architecture was "re-discovered" during the Renaissance, many artists and architects tried to illustrate the verbal descriptions contained in it. One of the most famous is by Leonardo da Vinci (adapted here in a drawing by William B. C. Harroff). It is based on Vitruvius' observation that a man's height is equal to his outstretched arms, and that if he lies on his back spread-eagled, a compass with one point placed on his navel would describe a circle that touched the bottoms of his feet and the tips of his hands. This bolstered architects' arguments that buildings should be based on the circle and square. It was a concept which fit nicely with the Christian view that God, as Great Architect, had designed the Universe with square and compass. (Compare this illustration with the French 13th century manuscript at the beginning of this book.)

THE RENAISSANCE

By the end of the 14th century, humanist studies had lead artists and scholars in Italy to conclude that culture had been in a constant decline since Roman times. They called the Middle Ages dark and barbaric (the original meaning for "gothic"), and they believed that only an intensive study of what the ancient Greeks and Romans had written -- Humanism- could restore civilization to its earlier heights. They treated the pagan philosophers much like Old Testament prophets who needed only to be "translated" into a Christian context to make them acceptable. The result of these efforts to Christianize pagan philosophy was a rebirth of CLASSICAL learning, art and architecture: the Renaissance

The Renaissance Man had a new outlook on his relationship to the universe. He had inherited the medieval definition of man as less than God, but he had added the rediscovered Greek definition of man being greater than animals or barbarians. The synthesis produced a new sense of dignity for man: he should explore his capabilities while recognizing his limitations. Man became the measure of **all** things.

At first, the Humanist scholars felt that the the achievements of the ancients could only be rediscovered, not surpassed. But during the course of the 15th century they realized that they had indeed surpassed the ancients in many ways. They began to believe the human intellect was capable of anything. The modern spirit of scientific inquiry was established.

Architects and artists, as Humanist scholars, studied the ruins of ancient Roman architecture carefully. CLASSICAL buildings and writings lead them to believe that all architecture must be based on the purest possible geometrical forms and mathematical relationships rather than on the irregular forms and exaggerated proportions of medieval architecture. They also believed that the Orders had been degraded and should be returned to the antique models.

THE EARLY RENAISSANCE

The first Renaissance building, The Foundling Hospital, (also called the Hospital of the Innocents) was built between 1419 and 1424, by Brunelleschi, a goldsmith by training. He had gone to Rome to study the ruins of ancient Roman buildings. In order to record them, he and a friend appear to have invented PERSPECTIVE, a means for giving the illusion of depth, of three dimensions, on a flat surface. (This innovation not only revolutionized the study and representation of architecture, it completely changed painting.) Brunelleschi was convinced from his studies that he could solve the most embarrassing problem facing the Florentines: how to complete the dome on their cathedral (the Duomo).

Typical Gothic competition between cities had inspired the Florentines to build a cathedral larger than any of their neighbors. They succeeded, but had built the base for a dome so large (nearly the diameter of the Pantheon and springing from a DRUM 18 stories above ground) that for a hundred years no one could figure out how to construct it -- there was not enough wood around to build the necessary centering and the walls were too thin to bear much weight. The Pantheon had convinced Brunelleschi that the dome could be built. He built up a series of ribs and panels in concentric rings, without centering, to create a light, double-shelled dome. In spirit, the dome was a Renaissance achievement even though its ribs, panels and pointed shape (to reduce outward thrusts on the walls) were Gothic.

The Foundling Hospital was designed by Brunelleschi shortly after he began the dome. It is entirely CLASSICAL in feeling, however, even though the inspiration seems to have come from local Romanesque buildings (like San Miniato al Monte) which Brunelleschi thought at the time were ancient Roman structures. Brunelleschi's succeeding designs became increasingly Roman in detail, and works like the church of Santo Spirito exceed most of the antique prototypes in their rigorous and rational use of geometry.

In Santo Spirito, Brunelleschi attempts to return the medieval Latin Cross plan to what he thought of as the purity of the Early Christian basilica. The nave is built up of multiples of the square crossing bay; the aisles are quarters of this MODULE and the vol-

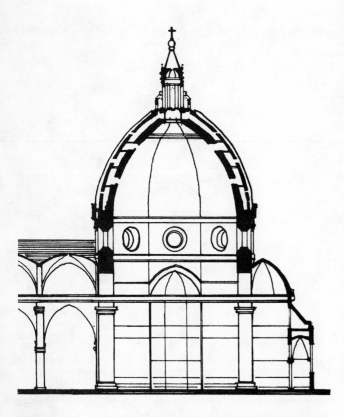

DUOMO   **section thru double-shelled dome**

umes of the church are cubes of space based on the crossing module and its subdivisions. The extension of whole from part is so consistent and logical that the entire church can be predicted from observing one bay. This is an intellectual philosophy of design which could be emotionally lifeless. Brunelleschi makes it tranquil, poetic, beautiful and satisfying.

Vitruvius was one of the ancient writers discovered by the Humanists. (Rediscovered by scholars, actually, since copies of Vitruvius were to be found in monastery libraries across Europe where they seem to have been continually consulted by architects and builders.) Several Renaissance Humanist-architects wrote new treatises on architecture based on Vitruvius. One of the best known of these is De re aedificatoria (the title in English is usually translated Ten Books on Architecture just as Vitruvius' book is) by another Florentine, Leon Battista Alberti. It was widely distributed after it was written because it was the first book on architecture to have been printed on the newly developed printing press. Alberti attempts to bring Vitruvius up to date technologically, although he accepts the Roman author as the authority for most aesthetic standards.

Although not trained as an architect, Alberti prepared designs for several buildings to illustrate his theories. In the Tempio Malatestiano in Rimini, Alberti designed a facade for an existing church which used the Roman triumphal arch as its basis, a design concept which would be extremely influential. At Santa Maria Novella in Florence, Alberti devised a scheme for integrating a triumphal arch MOTIF on the lower half of the facade with a temple-front motif on the top. Besides the references to antique buildings, this composition appealed to architects because it unified the ungainly projection on the facade of the high nave and low side aisles of the typical basilica. Alberti used huge volutes to tie the temple motif to the triumphal arch. This solution was widely imitated for centuries.

THE HIGH RENAISSANCE

Florence had been the cradle of the Early Renaissance during the 1400s (quattrocento). The immense wealth generated by its industries, trade and banking institutions had provided the means to build the

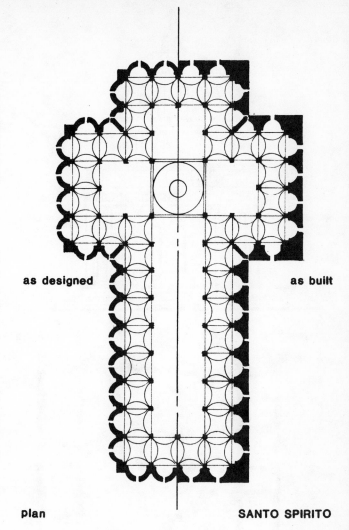

as designed   as built

plan   SANTO SPIRITO

elevation   SANTA MARIA NOVELLA

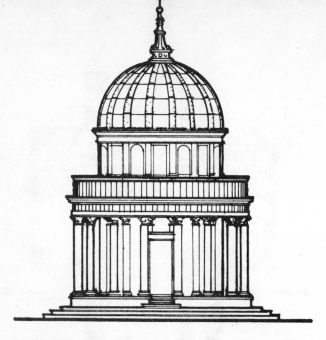

TEMPIETTO   **elevation**

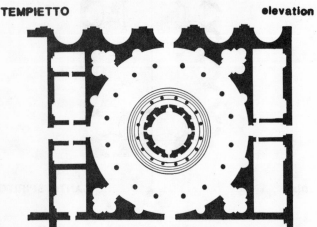

TEMPIETTO   **plan including courtyard**

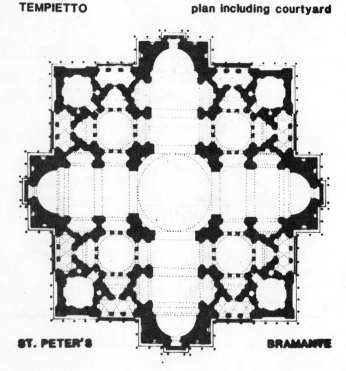

ST. PETER'S   **BRAMANTE**

Humanist-architects' designs. By the 1500s, however, the Papacy had returned to Rome from its ignominious exile in Avignon (the "Babylonian Captivity", 1309-77) and recovered much of its wealth and power. The Papacy began to rebuild Rome in a fashion which befitted its new prestige, and it became the natural center for the next stage of the Renaissance, the High Renaissance.

The building which best typifies the High Renaissance, its "high-water mark", is the Tempietto by Bramante. It is a small, centralized, church in part because it is a martyrium; it marks the spot where, according to tradition, St. Peter was crucified. But it is also designed as a perfectly circular building with a hemispherical dome set in a perfectly circular courtyard which in turn is inscribed in a square because this "perfect" geometry had become the goal of the Renaissance architect:

> "...the most beautiful and most regular forms ..are the circle and square....we, who know not false Gods...will choose the circle [for our temples]; for it alone is simple, uniform, equal, strong, and adapted to its purpose. Thus we should make our Temples circular,... most apt to demonstrate the Unity, the infinite Essence, the Uniformity and Justice of GOD."
> Palladio

Bramante had the opportunity to apply the same sort of centralized planning on a much larger scale when he was commissioned by Pope Julius II to replace the badly deteriorated Constantinian basilica of St. Peter's. He proposed an immense centralized structure entirely composed of squares and circles. The general plan was a Greek Cross in a large square. Smaller-scaled versions of the plan filled in the areas between the outer square and the arms of the cross, and the crossing itself was to have been covered by a hemispherical dome. The complex organization of the many spaces along cross-axes is reminiscent of the great Roman baths.

Foundations for Bramante's church were built and the corner piers constructed, but Bramante's death, the crumbling of the undersized piers and the Sack of Rome by troops of the Holy Roman Emperor brought construction to a halt. It took decades for the the morale and the finances of the Papacy to recover from the assault. Finally, the great Michelangelo was brought in to finish St. Peter's.

Michelangelo, already 71 years old when he under-
took the commission, brilliantly simplified Bramante's
scheme. Although he retained Bramante's plan in outline, his conception of the building and its geometry
is quite new. Instead of a series of interlocking
spaces arranged along axes, Michelangelo conceives
of the church as a sculptural whole. He organizes the
plan by superimposing geometries one on top of another rather than juxtaposing units. The spaces inside
the building flow into each other, and on the outside,
the wall seems to undulate around the interior
shapes. Michelangelo uses giant PILASTERS which
extend the full height of the facades instead of superimposing several Orders. The resulting vertical
expression carries up into the dome, also designed by
Michelangelo. The sense of continuous build-up to the
climax of the dome seems more gothic in character
than Renaissance, even though the individual details
of the building are all classical in inspiration.
Michelangelo has introduced a new dynamism and
expressivity into the architectural vocabulary.

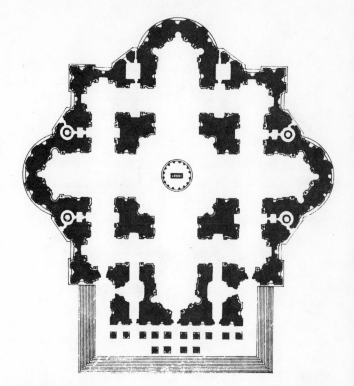

MICHELANGELO   **ST. PETER'S**

MANNERISM

Michelangelo and his equally great contemporaries
Raphael (the most famous painter of the time) and
Leonardo da Vinci (the universal Renaissance genius)
seemed so brilliant to most contemporaries, that artists worked in their shadows for decades, creating
works which many critics saw to be "in the manner"
of these giants. The Sack of Rome, destructive and
morally devastating (the effect can be compared to
that of World War I on Europe), combined with the
influence of these giants to produce an art and architecture which reflects the unease, the questioning of
values, of the time. Some historians call this art and
architecture Mannerist. The rules of design laid down
by Alberti and others were "disrespectfully" turned
upside down. Parts of buildings are ambiguously related to other parts; proportions are exaggerated;
unstable compositions are created. A definitive example of this kind of architecture is the Palazzo del Te
in Mantua, by Giulio Romano.

PALAZZO del TE   **partial elevation**

CITY PLANNING IN ROME

The rebuilding of St. Peter's basilica as the largest and most resplendent church in Christianity was only a part of a campaign to restore the entire city of Rome to its former Imperial glory. The barbarian invasions and removal of the capital to Constantinople had reduced Rome from a city of over a million inhabitants to a miserable community of perhaps 15,000 huddled together on the banks of the Tiber River. Except for the Pantheon and several basilicas built by Constantine, the ancient Roman buildings had been abandoned; they were too dispersed over the ruined city and too expensive to repair or maintain.

Since Rome had shrivelled rather than grown up around a core, she had no central, civic square. Although there had been an attempt in the 12th century to make the Capitoline Hill (Campidoglio), the hill overlooking the center of ancient Rome, into such a square, the idea failed to arouse civic pride until the 16th century when Michelangelo was commissioned to tidy up the existing city hall and the area immediately around it. This was a disorderly patchwork of buildings, the city hall (Palace of the Senators) having built piecemeal on the foundations of the Roman hall of records. For reasons of economy, Michelangelo was to design only a new facade for the Palace of the Senators and level the area in front for a public square (piazza). He prepared plans, however, which expanded the commission to include two additional facades for buildings flanking the square and a flight of stairs which linked the square to the city below.

Michelangelo's plans, which were completed after his death, created a square which was unified by a single design concept which related all three facades. The facades of the buildings to the sides of the piazza are understated and designed to focus attention on the city hall and its magnificent staircase. In fact, it is the space of the piazza which has become primary, not the buildings. The Campidoglio is a civic living room with the facades of buildings as its walls, not a mere space between buildings, as most city squares were (and are). Michelangelo also very cleverly transformed a problem into a positive attribute: a building existed on one side of the square which was set at an angle to the facade of the Palace of the Senators. Instead of relating the two buildings or-

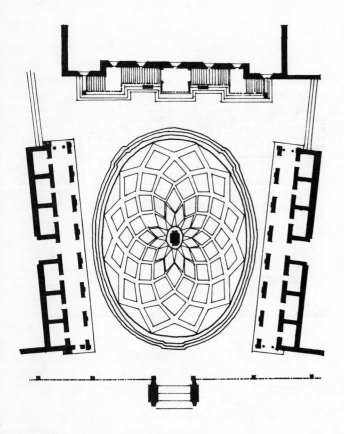

CAPITOLINE HILL   **plan**

thogonally, Michelangelo retained the angle between the building with his new facade and sited the opposite one at the same angle. This made the new piazza trapezoidal instead of rectangular, but the angles are slight enough that the visitor doesn't perceive them. As a result, the normal sensation of parallel horizontal lines converging, the phenomenon upon which perspective drawing is based, is reversed. The facade of the Senators' Palace is subjectively brought toward the viewer and made more important. The Giant Orders (Orders which extend through two or more stories, like those Michelangelo had already used on St. Peter's) add to the sense of grandeur, and a oval pattern for the paving of the piazza reinforces both the dynamism of the space and fits nicely into the trapezoidal shape of the piazza without calling attention to the angled relationships of the three facades. The ideas introduced into the Campidoglio were brilliantly innovative and effective. They would be elaborated by architects for centuries.

Like the rebuilding of St. Peter's, the Campidoglio was an isolated attack on Rome's decay. Pope Sixtus V replanned Rome in its entirety and managed to execute enough of his plan during his short, five-year reign, that it directed the growth and rebuilding of Rome to the present day. He was, in this respect, the first large-scale cityplanner since antiquity. Sixtus did not concentrate on building monuments (although he completed Michelangelo's unfinished project for the dome of St. Peter's in a mere 22 months); he concentrated on building a system of streets to connect existing monuments.

The scattering of the great Christian monuments throughout Rome (the Pantheon, the Colosseum -- both long since turned into religious shrines -- and several Constantinian and Medieval basilicas) discouraged pilgrims from visiting them. Paths to them wandered through overgrown ruins where the pilgrims were subject to attacks by bands of roving criminals. All of this was bad for the image of Rome (and equally bad for the economy since tourists then as now spent a lot of money).

Sixtus erected one of the Egyptian obelisks which had been brought to Rome during the Empire in front of each of the major churches. He then drew straight lines connecting the monuments on a map and commanded workers to level the paths between them, cutting hills where necessary and filling in valleys. He also proposed or created fountains where roads

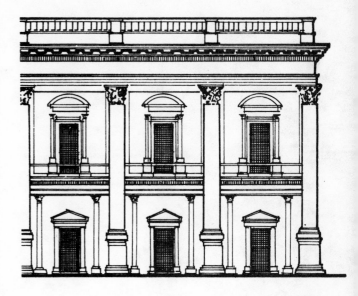

partial side elevation　　　CAPITOLINE HILL

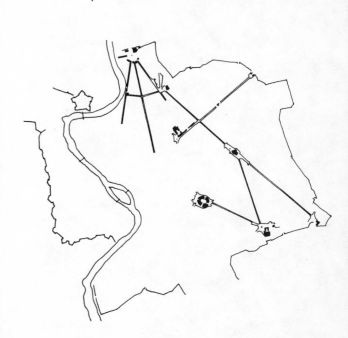

SIXTUS V's PLANNING of ROME

intersected or widened. The resulting network was so powerful both in image and in form that it could not be ignored, and it directed all future development in the city. Sixtus also reinforced his planning concepts by eliminating the bands of brigands, creating new industries, giving parcels of land for development and proposing social housing, all modern-appearing attitudes.

BAROQUE ARCHITECTURE

The Sack of Rome by the troops of Charles V was only one of two nearly simultaneous blows to the Roman Catholic Church. The other, the Protestant Reformation, would have the greater long-term effects on the Church. For the first time since the Fall of the Roman Empire, the Pope was not the undisputed spiritual leader of the West. Centuries of bitter fighting between Catholics and Protestants began, some of it waged by armies and some of it through propaganda. The Catholic Church became sensitive to the charges of the Reformers. One of the criticisms concerned religious art and architecture: it had become too worldly and so dryly intellectual that the average worshipper couldn't understand or appreciate it.

Patron, priest and artist alike sensed a way out of this dilemma in the dynamism and emotional appeal which Michelangelo had pioneered in his art and architecture. Over the period of a century, the pure intellectualism of Renaissance theory and practice gave way to a more sensuous (and occasionally sensual) art. The oval replaced the circle as a favored form, and the diagonal replaced the vertical and horizontal; instead of static balance in their compositions, artists and architects tried to communicate a sense of movement. They tried to make their buildings more intriguing, more dramatic, by linking spaces together in sequences and by using techniques developed for the theater.

The greatest of these theatrical sequences was that designed by Bernini for St. Peter's. A great space was needed in front of St. Peter's both to give it some visual relief from the medieval buildings which crowded up against it and to hold the tens of thousands of faithful who came to hear the Pope speak from a balcony on the facade. The relatively undis-

tinguished facade of the church was overpowering in
its monumentality; and the interior, which had been
greatly enlarged by the addition of a nave to Michelangelo's crossing, apse and transepts, was austere by
the standards of the time. (The nave had been added
because the post-Reformation clergy found the centralized plan incompatible with Catholic ceremony.)
The sequence Bernini designed to alleviate these
problems began with a double colonnade that curves
around an oval piazza of grandiose dimensions. The
columns are arranged to prevent direct views into
the piazza. A visitor has only tantalizing glimpses
through it. Once he has penetrated the colonnade,
its curving wings sweep his eyes around to a break in
the long side of the oval, an opening which gives
onto a smaller, trapezoidal piazza in front of the
facade. (The opening in the colonnade toward the
city was made under Mussolini in the 1930s and
weakens the effect of enclosure and surprise intended by Bernini.)

Bernini could not create one large space in front of
St. Peter's because the palace of the Pope would
have projected into it. He turns this limitation to his
advantage, much as Michelangelo had in the Campidoglio. In fact, by placing the major gathering area
at some distance from the facade, Bernini diminishes
its overpowering scale and allows Michelangelo's
dome to be appreciated. The crowd in the oval piazza is now fairly far away from the Pope at his balcony on the facade, but Bernini makes him **seem** closer to the crowd by using the same reverse perspective device which Michelangelo had introduced in the
Campidoglio.

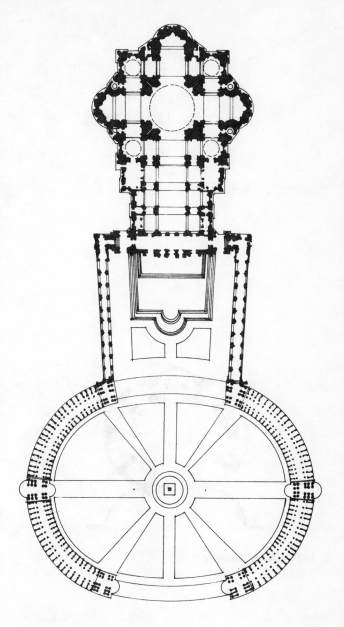

CHURCH and PIAZZA   **ST. PETER'S**

The sequence of discoveries and screened views is
continued by Bernini inside St. Peter's. He designed a
great baldachino, a bronze, canopy-like, martyrium
under the dome and over the spot which marks the
supposed grave of St. Peter. This ten-story high
structure not only dramatizes the crossing, it also
serves as a frame, a proscenium arch, for the blaze
of gilded bronze (a sculpture by Bernini) that cele-
brates the "throne of St. Peter" at the very end of
the apse, more than 200 feet beyond the opening of
the baldachino.

Among Bernini's other additions to St. Peter's was
the Scala Regia (Royal Stairs), his most theatrical. It
connects the end of the vestibule of St. Peter's with
the Pope's private apartments. The stairs are not not
very long in reality, but Bernini makes them look

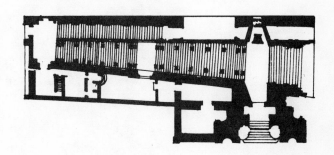

SCALA REGIA

grand by forcing the perspective: instead of the walls of the staircase being parallel, they converge toward the top of the stairs and the ceiling slopes down as it rises. The sense of depth is exaggerated, and the stairs looks magnificent -- unless someone stands near the its top and destroys the illusion. It is no wonder that Bernini was famous as a set designer as well as architect and sculptor, for this forced perspective is the sort of device still used to make shallow sets look deep. (See, for example, the permanent sets in Palladio's Teatro Olimpico in Vicenza.)

Bernini makes full use of theatrical devices in the small, but effective church of Sant' Andrea al Quirinale. The oval plan, with its long axis parallel to the street makes the interior seem expansive. The setting off of the altar behind a "proscenium" into an area with its own, hidden, lighting transforms the sanctuary into an auditorium for sacred theater. The eye is lead diagonally up from a painting of the crucifixion of St. Andrew above the altar to a sculpture of the Saint rising to heaven in a break of the pediment over the proscenium and on to the golden light streaming through the LANTERN in the white and gilded dome. This is a bravura ensemble that is emotionally and spiritually convincing, if, as the Baroque artist requires, the participant is willing "to suspend disbelief" for a moment. The Renaissance artists asks the observer to understand his work intellectually but from an emotional distance; the Baroque artist asks the observer to become emotionally involved in, to participate in his work.

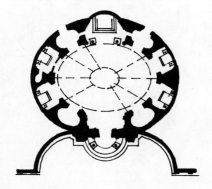

S. ANDREA AL QUIRNALE

BAROQUE AND ROCOCO OUTSIDE ITALY

Painters, sculptors and architects from the rest of Europe went to Rome to study the forms and concepts which Bernini and other Italian masters introduced. In southern Germany hundreds of beautiful churches used these Baroque devices to appeal to Germans who had strayed from the Catholic church during the Reformation. A good example is the church at Rohr by the Asam brothers. The plain exterior in no way prepares one for the lavish interior. With their illusionism and decoration, the Asams created an an enchanting "other world" for the peasant to worship in. By using a proscenium arch-framed altar composition (as Bernini did in S. Andrea), concealed lighting, and a statue of the Virgin Mary with no apparent means of support, the Asams give the illusion of the Virgin rising from her coffin into heaven. This is religious theater of the most appealing and effective kind.

Although the French also sent their painters and architects to Rome to study, French Baroque architecture is much less exuberant, much more restrained and rational than its Italian prototypes (or German equivalents). French culture was entering the Age of Reason, (the Enlightenment), which could be characterized by a phrase of Descartes, one of the brilliant philosophers of the period: "Cogito ergo sum." (I think, therefore I am.) That is, all existence is predicated on the ability to think -- not on faith or belief. Even when French Baroque (especially in its later phase, the effusive Rococo) becomes elaborate, emotional appeal is usually subject to order and reason, if not intellect.

By the mid-1660s, France had become the most powerful political entity in the West. A series of French kings and their ministers began a process of centralizing power. When Louis XIV became king, he could state with no exaggeration: "I am the state." The modern national state had been created; Louis was the first absolutist ruler since antiquity. A new style of architecture was needed and was consciously sought to portray both the power of the king and the glory of France. It was inspired by Italian architecture, and translated unmistakably into something French. But it was conceived neither by nor for the King himself, but by his finance minister Fouquet.

Vaux-le-Vicomte was Fouquet's country estate, built to be near Louis XIV's palace at Fontainebleau and to impress the King, by its very lavishness, of his minister's brilliance. Fouquet assembled a team of young, untried, geniuses to design it. Le Vau (the architect), Le Brun (the interior designer) and Le Notre (the landscape architect) produced an ensemble of unprecedented splendor and unity. Le Notre reordered and geometrized nature into an interlocking grid of terraced gardens, pools and foliage -- even the trees were trimmed into rectangular shapes. The chateau (palace) itself was conceived, like the fountains and statues in the park, as an event in the grid, strung along great axes with other events like pearls on a string. The parts, the details of the whole ensemble at Vaux-le-Vicomte may be less dynamic than in a work by Bernini, but the total effect is equally theatrical: a gigantic, ordered, stage set where spectator is, in turn, actor.

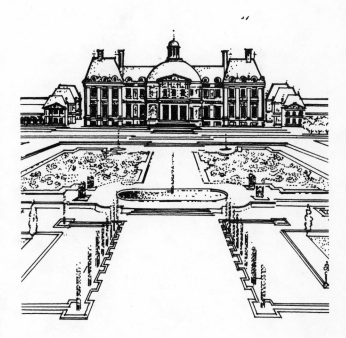

VAUX-LE-VICOMTE

King Louis was very impressed. He was impressed by the brilliant innovations of Fouquet and his designers, and he was impressed by the cost of the whole project. He deduced that his finance minister must have embezzled a great deal from him and had Fouquet thrown into prison for life. But he hired Fouquet's design team and set them to work on the his own country estate at Versailles, which he had them remodel into the capital of France.

Louis detested Paris, then the capital of France. He found it crowded, unsanitary and prone to revolt. (He had been forced to flee Paris from a revolt as a child, and he never forgot it -- or forgave Paris.) He had Le Vau-Le Brun-Le Notre expand his father's hunting chateau and gardens on the model of Vaux-le-Vicomte but at a scale appropriate to the most powerful individual in the Western World. The chateau, in its final form, could house at least 6,000 people, and Louis compelled most of the nobility of France to live in it, thereby breaking the last remnants of France's feudal structure.

Political power radiated both really and symbolically from Louis' person in the chateau. He was, appropriately, nicknamed the "Sun King." The sun was symbolized everywhere in the plan: three broad avenues radiate from the King's bedroom into the city that was built on one side of the chateau and the gardens are replete with sun-burst patterns of paths. The main axis of the complex was arranged so that the path of the sun represented the contemporary theory that the universe was made of four elements: earth, fire, air and water. This axis was oriented east-west so that the sun (Louis/fire) rose in the hills (earth), passed through the air and set over the Grand Canal (water). Virtually every piece of decoration; every painting, sculpture or tapestry was designed to flatter Louis and contribute to his myth.

Such an immense undertaking, combined with the desires of the design team, demanded the establishment of art and architecture schools -- the first in history -- and factories to train designers and artisans to produce the furnishings needed for chateau and gardens. Through these schools, Louis as effectively centralized control over the arts as he had over the people and his nobles.

VERSAILLES

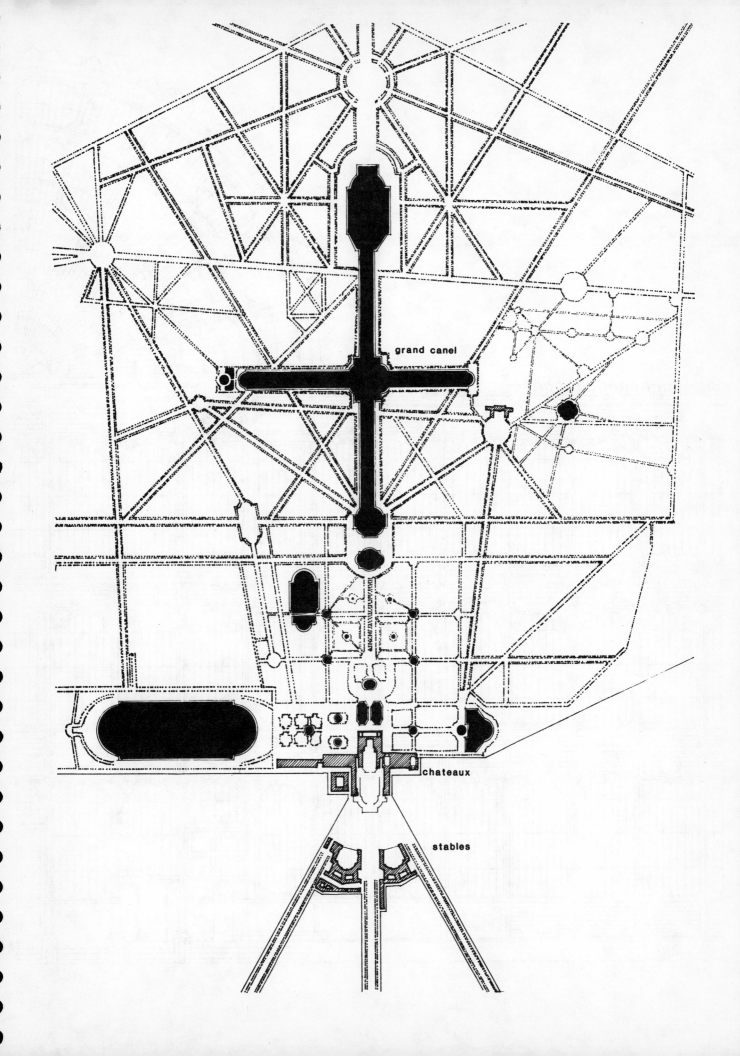

grand canel

chateaux

stables

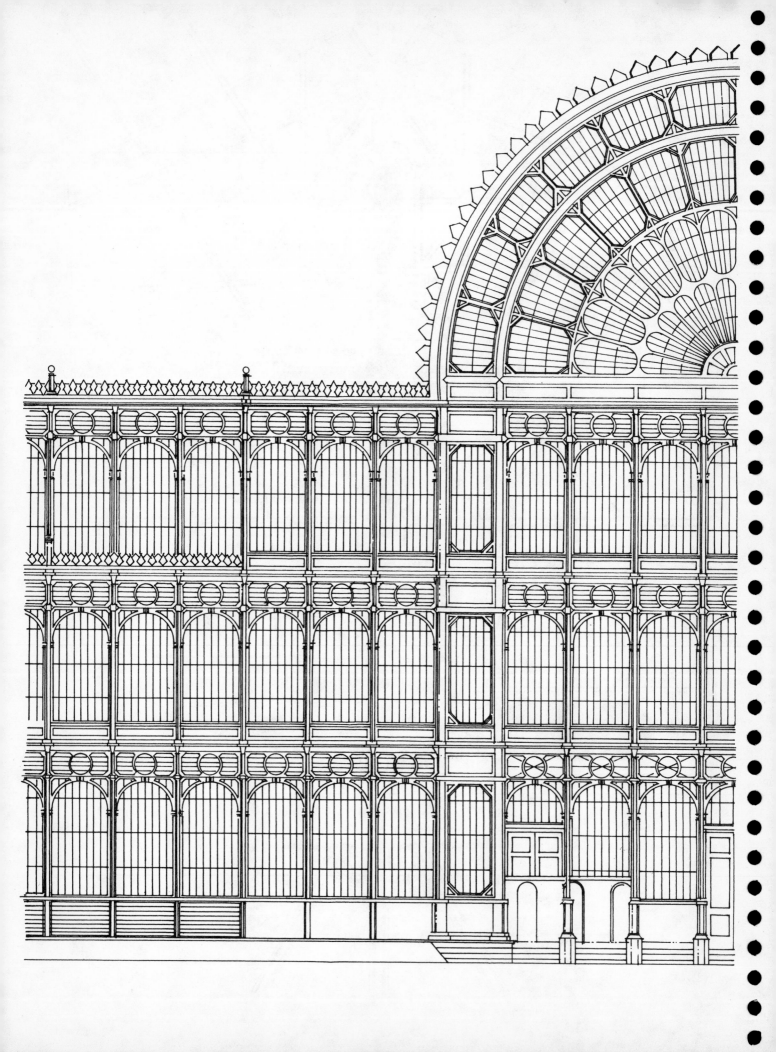

MODERN ARCHITECTURE

PARTIAL ELEVATION OF THE CRYSTAL PALACE

The Crystal Palace, built for the Great Exposition of 1851 in London (the first world's fair), would certainly be on anyone's list of "The Most Important Monuments of Modern Architecture." Although designed by a gardener, Joseph Paxton, not an architect, there have been few public buildings so popular or influential. It was built almost entirely of standardized, factory-produced parts of iron and glass. The Crystal Palace entranced a public accustomed to heavy buildings of stone and brick and showed the possibilities, aesthetic as well as practical, of building with metal and glass.

THE MODERN AGE

THE AGE OF REVOLUTIONS

Louis XIV reigned 72 years. His style of government, art and architecture were imitated whenever possible. Paris and Versailles had replaced Rome and Florence as the centers of taste, culture, and intellectual matters. The King may have centralized control over the first two, but intellectual activities in France -- in the West in general -- began to take on a life of their own, a life which would eventually destroy the monarchy and create the basis of the modern world.

Age of Reason philosophies led to major scientific discoveries. Sir Isaac Newton's formulations of the Laws of Universal Gravitation and The Calculus, appeared to confirm the speculations of philosophers that man could understand the laws which governed the universe with his intellect rather than accept them on faith. If so, argued such great Enlightenment philosophers as Benjamin Franklin, man should be ruled by reason, by reasonable men, not by kings who had inherited their power. These philosophies lay behind the American "War of Independence" and a series of political revolutions in other countries beginning with The French Revolution of 1789.

The liberal, rationalist, scientific and humanitarian artists and philosophers of the age of revolutions rejected the sometimes frivolous, usually sensuous and light-hearted, Rococo style of architecture which was then popular at the time. They demanded a morally serious art and architecture, an art that would teach values and reflect intellectual advances. Few architects managed to bridge this gap between Enlightenment intellectualism and the emotional appeal of the Baroque. One was the Italian Guarini. A leading mathematician, he used forms and principles of the new mathematics (especially descriptive geometry) to create mystical drama in such buildings as Santissima Sindone (Church of the Holy Shroud) and San Lorenzo in Turin. More characteristic of the new style that was emerging out of the Enlightenment are paintings such as J. L. David's "The Oath of the Horatii". It is relentlessly austere in form and composition, morally uplifting in its message.

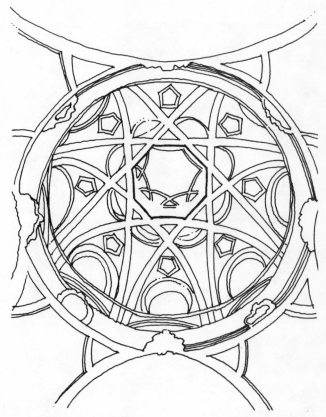

view up into the dome

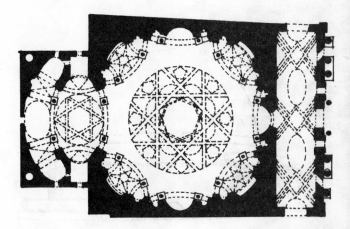

plan   SAN LORENZO

Even more rigorously classical than David's painting is the monument to the intellectual hero of the Enlightenment, Sir Isaac Newton. Designed by Boulée, the Newton Cenotaph was a pure product of the intellect. It could never have been built. Boulée intended the great sphere to symbolize the universe, whose laws Newton had discovered. The surface of the sphere was to have been pierced by holes arranged like the constellations. Sunlight would have turned the interior into a planetarium centuries before the fact. In plan, the project is a series of concentric circles, a schematic of the solar system. Every form and detail, even the unclimbable stairs leading to a ring of cypresses (an ancient symbol for eternity), derived from this circular geometry. Compared to the Baroque, Boulée and his compatriots had returned to the classicism of Bramante's Tempietto, thus the new style is sometimes referred to as "Neoclassicism."

The contrasts between Rococo confection and Neoclassical puritanism parallel the political tensions between the supernumerary, pleasure-loving, aristocracy and the intellectual community, tensions which were released explosively in the severing of aristocrat's head from body during the French Revolution of 1789.

In England, the Age of Reason led to an industrial rather than a political revolution. Why The Industrial Revolution did not begin earlier is difficult to explain. Virtually all of the necessary technology and theory had been around since Hellenistic times. In any case, three interrelated phenomena lay behind the revolution: the development of the steam engine (and railroad); the exploitation of coal as a source of cheap energy for the steam engines; and the production of iron in large quantities (which in turn required the cheap energy of coal). These three things made possible the factory system and the transportation network necessary for distributing raw materials and finished goods. They revolutionized finance, culture, art, and nearly every other aspect of society as much or more than the political revolutions. Both, in reality, are different manifestations of the same philosophical revolution.

The effects of the Industrial Revolution on architecture were immediate and profound. With industrialization comes urbanization and all of the new types of buildings and structures associated with a big city:

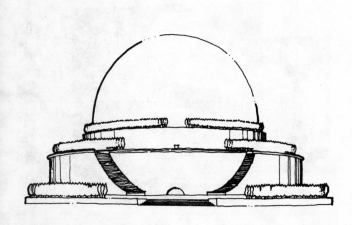

THE NEWTON CENOTAPH

factories, railroad stations, office buildings, hospitals, warehouses, department stores, and so on. With industrialization came new building materials and technologies for the architect: iron, steel, reinforced concrete, aluminum and glass in large sizes and quantities. With industrialization came the pumps and motors that made very tall and very large buildings possible.

At first, the professional architect resisted using the new materials and designing buildings for industry. Historical precedent had become extremely important for him, and there was no historical precedent for the new building types. The architect had worked hard since the Middle Ages to make architecture a profession: he considered industry "beneath" his high social position. As the 19th century wore on, however, it became obvious to a larger and larger group of architects that industrialization was unavoidable -- and the source of the big commissions in the future. By the turn of the 20th century, architects were coming to include industrial materials, and even industrial forms, in most of their buildings.

The introduction of the new materials occurred in such apparently unobtrusive structures as bridges. The Ironbridge at Coalbrookdale, built in 1777-79 by Abraham Darby II and a local architect, demonstrated the potentials of the iron from Darby's nearby mills, the first to produce iron on a large scale. Ironbridge was an unimpressive, by today's standards, 100 foot span. It was constructed as if it were made of wood. But it appeared light and airy to contemporaries and excited many with the possibilities of this type of construction. Many projects for bridges in iron appeared in the following years, and they showed the spirit of competition which characterizes the Industrial Age. Larger and larger spans were attempted, and techniques which took better advantage of iron were introduced. Foremost among these was the suspension bridge.

Suspension bridges take advantage of the tensile strength of wrought iron or steel (see p. 9 above); by suspending the roadway from cables or chains that are hung across the tops of towers, (instead of holding up the roadway with columns or trusses) incredible spans may be achieved. Within 50 years of the Ironbridge, the Clifton Suspension Bridge, near Bristol, England, had spanned 900 feet between supports. The Brooklyn Bridge in New York had reached 1,595 feet by 1867, and the current record span is the Ver-

COALBROOKDALE   **IRON BRIDGE**

azzano Narrows Bridge in New York which stretches 4260 feet between supports. In addition, the curves of the cables or chains is not the arbitrary choice of the designer; these curves must follow the laws of nature. With the suspension bridge, form does not follow some abstract theory of design, it is dictated by the nature of the materials from which the structure is made.

This idea, that architectural form should be dictated by the nature of the building problem itself, was relatively new. It's ramifications on architectural theory continued to expand for the next century. Warehouses and factories were built that were purely functional and solidly constructed but completely undecorated. Vitruvius' criteria of Firmness and Commodity were satisfied, but was there delight? Many of these utilitarian buildings did have a sort of raw beauty to them; the idea that a functional form could be beautiful without being decorated began to be discussed.

Other "functional" buildings, such as greenhouses, introduced new and intriguing forms and architectural effects which captivated by their novelty and in some respects redefined the traditional concepts of beauty and structure. In the Palm Stove at Kew Gardens (just outside London), for example, the old relationship between carrier and carried is negated by the soap-bubble surface of glass. Its weightless appearance and the alternately reflective and transparent nature of the glass, the ability to see through its walls, fascinated the public and architects alike.

Greenhouse construction inspired a variety of buildings among which were sheds of vast extent built to cover the platforms of the new railroad stations. The hotels and entries in front of the trainsheds often were conceived as quite traditional buildings, however, and illustrate the separation between architect and engineer that was developing.

Even more spectacular and influential than the trainsheds was the Crystal Palace, the building housing London's Great Exposition of 1851, the first world's fair. It's designer, Paxton, was a gardener, but he had designed a number of greenhouses. He utilized the same technologies of standard-sized, interchangeable parts which could be machine-made to build the immense (1851 feet long) exhibition building. The glass and iron structure was built in a mere nine months. Paxton had not only introduced the all-glass

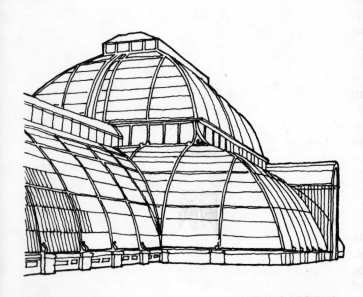

PALM STOVE   **KEW GARDENS**

building, he had virtually invented the assembly-line technique of using prefabricated (factory-made parts) to do it. The building was a popular success and has influenced architects to the present (Phillip Johnson's Crystal Cathedral in California, is a recent descendant).

ROMANTICISM

From its very beginnings, the side effects of industrialization (destruction of the agrarian economy; the creation of huge, dirty, ugly, industrial cities with horrible slums and the exploitation of the working class) had disturbed many. One reaction was Romanticism,the "escape to the distant in time or space." Romantic literature described the mythical, the exotic, and the medieval (Sir Walter Scott's Ivanhoe, for example). There was an architectural counterpart. James Wyatt, for example, built Fonthill Abbey, an immense evocation of a gothic monastery where the eccentric Englishman William Beckford could have parties. John Nash built the Brighton Pavilion, a fantastic concoction of architectural motifs from India and Arabia. Ancient Greece also appealed. Leo von Klenze built Valhalla, a romantic copy of a Greek temple, on the hills near Regensburg, Germany.

BRIGHTON PAVILION

THE ARTS AND CRAFTS MOVEMENT

Only the wealthy, the very industrialists who were causing the problems, could afford to escape from the ugly side of the Industrial Revolution into an architectural fantasyworld of gothic castles, but the attention which Romantic literature and architecture gave to the Middle Ages led another group of artists and writers to directly attack the Industrial Revolution. The architect Pugin published a series of satirical drawings which showed the same town as it had been during the Middle Ages and as it had become. The Medieval cities were beautiful, the people happy and healthy; the modern cities were ugly and polluted, the people starving and miserable. His point, expanded by John Ruskin (the most famous art critic of the Victorian Age), was that industrialization had destroyed society, that machine production in factories intrinsically reduced men to machines, destroying their pride and individuality in the process. Men should return to the Medieval handicraft practices.

The poor aesthetic quality of machine-made products destroyed the tastes and morals of the people who bought them as much as of the men and women who produced them.

The Arts and Crafts group justified such conclusions by pointing to contemporary industrial products and art. Ruskin and his follower William Morris condemned these products as "dishonest". Brick should look like brick and not be covered over with plaster (as was contemporary practice); plaster should not be made to look like stone (what would they have thought of wood-grained plastics?); decorative patterns on rugs and wallpapers should look flat, not give the illusion of depth. In sum, materials and designs should be "fit for their purpose."

The conclusions that artist and architects should return to the medieval techniques of handcrafting were unrealistic and influenced few people. By the time these assertions were made, it was obvious that industrialization was inevitable. But the other conclusions of the Arts and Crafts group were widely influential, particularly the concept of "fitness for purpose;" and the generalization that art and architecture were not only an expression of the moral values of a society, but also could actually shape those values was one of the most potent artistic theories introduced in the 19th century.

RED HOUSE

The linking of art and architecture with social questions was being developed by Ruskin, Morris and their followers at the same time Karl Marx was writing the Communist Manifesto. Indeed, William Morris, the leading designer of the Arts and Crafts Movement, was an avid and active supporter of the socialist movement. He declared that "there shouldn't be art for the few any more than freedom for the few," and proposed an art for the masses. Unfortunately for his theories, the handcrafting process he advocated was prohibitively expensive, and only the rich bourgeoisie could afford his creations. (He never did resolve this irony.) He was wealthy enough to put his theories into practice, however, in his own house, the Red House at Bexleyheath (near London). Its plain red-brick construction and an exterior form which corresponded exactly to the functional plan demonstrated his principles of "honesty" in design. Its furnishings, all designed and fabricated by Morris and his friends were paragons of the Arts and Crafts ideal of "fitness for purpose."

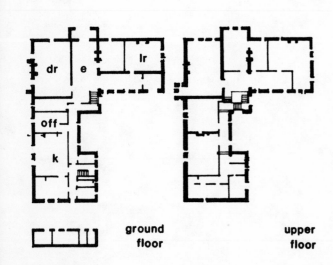

ground floor   upper floor

RED HOUSE

ECLECTICISM EVOLUTION AND ARCHITECTURE

Romanticism and the Arts and Crafts Movement represent only two of the many directions architecture took in the 19th century; engineers represent a third direction. Escape from the Industrial Age, opposition to the Industrial Age, and uncritical acceptance of it. Never had the architecture of an era shown such a wide diversity of approach. As you may well imagine, these are the extreme approaches; most of the architecture built lay somewhere between these directions. Most architecture used some details of architecture from the past and some engineering details: buildings with, say, gothic windows inserted into facades that looked Byzantine or Romanesque and used iron and glass construction for skylights and attached greenhouses. This mixture of details from various periods is called Eclecticism and was, in fact, the dominant mode of architectural design in the 19th century. It was considered "modern" by most. After all, it showed that the modern architect was aware of all the past styles and was sophisticated enough to choose the most appropriate detail and technique for the task at hand.

Some architects and critics from all of the above groups were not content merely to copy the architecture of the past, however. They argued that a totally new architectural expression, independent of the past, should be developed for the industrial age. They argued that the styles of the past had been developed without the advantage of iron, glass and the other modern materials; they argued that the past had never had to face most of the types of buildings which existed in the present and that past forms were therefore inappropriate. Until the end of the century, however, no critic or architect could propose a satisfactory new style for the "modern age," and in practice these architects lapsed into one sort of eclectic style or the other.

Nonetheless, the demands for a new style were buttressed by scientific developments, notably Darwin's theory of evolution, which he published in his Origin of the Species. Architectural theorists, following upon the evolutionists, argued that if man and society had evolved, then architecture, as a reflection of society, should also evolve. The "New Architecture" should not look like the historical styles and should be superior to them.

The Frenchman, Viollet-le-Duc, probably the greatest architectural theorist of the 19th century, offered a counter-argument in his Lectures on Architecture (Entretiens sur l'Architecture). He pointed out that he like most of his contemporaries believed the Parthenon had never been excelled as a piece of architecture and that the gothic cathedrals were, on the whole, better buildings than virtually anything built in modern times. Thus, while not arguing against the theories of evolution as they applied to organic life, he concluded that the analogy between architecture and evolution was not valid nor reasonable: architecture had, demonstrably, **not** evolved during the history of man. What **was** common to great monuments of the past like the Parthenon or Chartres cathedral was the clear reason for being of every element in them; these masterpieces had responded to site, climate, and the highest level of technology available to their architects. On the basis of this reasoning Viollet, too, argued for a rationalist "New Architecture": one which respected the principles of history without copying details; one in which each detail was the evident and logical result of an analysis of the building program. He said that architectural forms should follow upon their functions without preconception or prejudice on the part of the architect. It was obvious to Viollet that a modern architect would use the latest engineering methods and the most recently developed building materials to achieve this end. Therefore, Viollet concluded, the New Architecture would be an architecture of iron construction openly expressed and designed to take maximum advantages of the strength of iron. Viollet, who was also the leading restorer of medieval buildings in Europe, realized that he was too steeped in Medieval architecture to find the appropriate forms for iron construction; it would take a younger architect, one with a fresher point of view.

ART NOUVEAU

Viollet's theories had managed to transcend the questions which had divided architecture into so many different stylistic streams. It respected and took into account the great architecture of the past without leading to servile copying; it potentially avoided questions of eclecticism; it reconciled engineering with architecture and it suggested that "style" would result from analysis of the architectural program. Most of the recognized masters of modern architecture based their theories in greater or lesser degree on Viollet's theories: Frank Lloyd Wright in the US, Gaudi in Spain, Le Corbusier in France. But it was a young Belgian, Victor Horta who first put Viollet's theories into practice in way so convincing that the style of architecture -- or at least the style of decoration -- he originated swept Europe for a short while and paved the way for the architecture of the 20th century.

In the Tassel House in Brussels (1893) Horta radically changed the concept of the townhouse by analyzing, without preconception, the needs of his client. He used an exposed iron skeleton to open completely Tassel's house, which was built on a very narrow, deep, city lot. The iron skeleton allowed him to create the "open plan" (plan libre) by eliminating most of the interior partitions (making the house seem larger than it was) and to introduce natural light into the center of the house through a large, glazed, skylit conservatory.

Horta created a new style of decoration for the house, Art Nouveau, which he felt was consistent both with the exposed iron columns and trusses and the plants in the conservatory/greenhouse. The curvilinear, whiplash, wrought-iron decorations at the tops of the iron columns in the conservatory were translated into paintings on walls and ceilings, mosaics on the floor and stained glass in windows and doors. It was this novel architectural decoration, similar to some contemporary book illustrations and wallpaper designs, which became immediately popular, not the structural and spatial innovations. Art Nouveau architects in general came to be criticized for being preoccupied with decoration; the "New Art" was, in most cases, being applied to a traditional concept of building as if it were another historical style. An architecture which satisfied critics as thoroughly new was formulated in the years just before the outbreak of World War I. In many respects, the catalyst for a really "new" architecture came from the New World, the United States.

TASSEL HOUSE

THE UNITED STATES

COLONIAL AND
INDIGENOUS ARCHITECTURE

The indigenous architecture which settlers found when they arrived in the New World bore little resemblance to the European traditions they had left, and the Europeans looked down on the Indians as "culturally inferior." Because sensitivity to nature is integral to their culture, however, the Indians had developed building traditions which responded superbly to the natural environment, to site, sun, wind and rain. Each tribe responded to the particular environmental conditions in which it lived in finding architectural forms which reflected its own cultural values. The cliff dwellings of the Southwest complement their sites instead of destroying them; they take maximum advantage of winter sun and summer breeze but protect from summer sun and winter winds. Thick walls moderate daily and seasonal swings of temperature. The pueblo achieves similar ends; but because of the differences of terrain and available materials, the resulting forms are quite different. The teepee of the Plains Indians was a sophisticated, portable "machine" for living that took maximum advantage of natural phenomena. We are only beginning to appreciate our native American architecture because of our own increasing respect for the environment and the rise in energy prices.

The early settlers paid scant attention to these adaptations, however, modelling their architecture on that of the regions in Europe from which they'd come. From time to time European architects were asked to send designs to the Colonies for important buildings. There were few professional architects among the colonists, and those few had been trained in Europe. Thus, until the latter part of the 19th century, architecture in the United States largely paralleled developments in Europe.

The dearth of trained architects was filled by craftsmen who frequently based their designs on illustrated

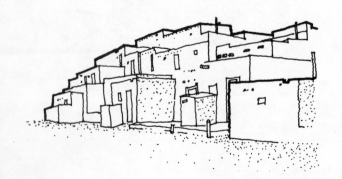

PUEBLO   **TAOS, NEW MEXICO**

books of the latest European buildings. These craftsmen unconsciously created a recognizable and unique
body of architecture, (which we loosely call Colonial
Architecture) when they used local materials and
techniques to execute these designs: a church
designed to be built of stone tends to achieve a
character of its own when built out of wood.

Thomas Jefferson was instrumental in trying to find a
style of architecture less dependent on European traditions and more expressive of the ideals of the new
republic. He was a genuine Renaissance man, a talented architect as well as a great writer, philosopher,
inventor and politician. His early training had been
informal, chiefly through books by English architects
that had been influenced by the 16th century Italian
architect Palladio. (Jefferson's own house, Monticello, was inspired by Palladio's Villa Rotunda but has
been utterly transformed by Jefferson's individual
genius.) After he was made ambassador to France,
however, he became acquainted with Enlightenment
architects and their works. Jefferson carried these
ideas back to the United States and developed them,
designing some of the finest buildings in the United
States (the Capitol at Richmond, Virginia, and the
University of Virginia among others). He believed that
Republican Rome should be the model for American
architecture just as it had been for American law. In
fact, Jefferson based his design for the capitol of
Virginia very closely on the Maison Carée at Nimes
(which he thought was a Republican Temple).

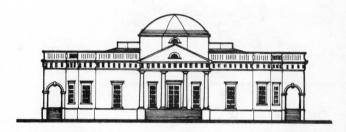

JEFFERSON   **MONTICELLO**

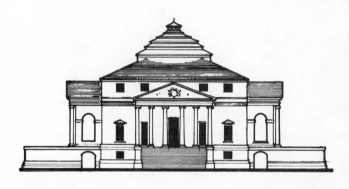

PALLADIO   **VILLA ROTUNDA**

WASHINGTON, D. C.

The decision to build a brand new capital city for
the United States forced the nation's leaders to make
a commitment to an appropriate American architecture. The site was chosen by George Washington and
a French engineer, Pierre L'Enfant, who had grown
up in Versailles. He proposed a city plan which was
an adaptation of Le Notre's gardens at Versailles.
The Capitol and President's house were to be located
on the most prominent hills. They would generate
axes and radiating street patterns which would define
the location of other major public buildings. Foreign
embassies were to line a mall directly analogous to
the main axis of the garden at Versailles.

Jefferson, on the other hand, wanted the plan of the
new Capital to be a rationalist grid. The final plan
was a compromise between Jefferson's and L'Enfant's

WASHINGTON   **D.C.**

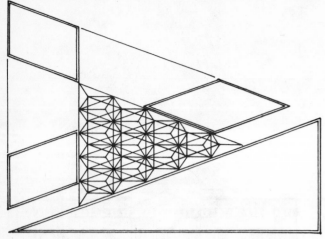

THE EAST WING

ideas. This plan still directs building in the Capital, although there have been some deviations over the centuries. There has been a tendency over the last couple of decades to respect L'Enfant's scheme and correct these deviations when possible. The East Wing addition to the National Gallery by I. M. Pei is an example of a contemporary building whose forms and locations were inspired by L'Enfant's original plan.

The first two public buildings for the new city were designed through competitions. The competition for the President's House (the "White House") was won by an amateur, James Hoban. His simple, handsome scheme strongly resembled contemporary European Neo-classical buildings and was criticized as too ostentatious by Jefferson (whose anonymous entry, based on the Villa Rotunda had lost). Another amateur, a physician, Dr. Thornton designed the Capitol. His project incorporated references to the Pantheon for the central part of the building with references to several "modern" French and English buildings in the Senate and House of Representative extensions to each side. Thornton's original design has been drastically modified over the years to accommodate the vast expansion of the country from the original 13 States. Most significant were the additions by Bulfinch early in the 19th century, and the enormous extensions (including the present cast-iron dome) that were made during the Civil War by Thomas U. Walter. (Both of these men were professionally trained architects.)

AMERICAN INNOVATIONS

The Neo-Classical architecture of the Capitol and White House, replete with classical Orders and other motifs from ancient Greece and Rome and from the Renaissance, did establish an "official" American style. It was emulated in capitol and court house across the United States. As the century wore on, this style was supplemented by the eclectic approach popular at the Ecole des Beaux Arts in Paris (the most influential school of architecture in the 19th century). For religious buildings, however, architects often turned to the revival of Medieval architecture which was then fashionable in Britain and on the Continent.

American domestic architecture showed more originality than government buildings and churches. In the

established Eastern cities, the more pretentious upper
class houses resembled their European counterparts,
but in the rapidly expanding frontier towns, unique
problems evolved a more purely American architecture. Houses needed to be built quickly; brick and
stone were often in short supply whereas wood was
plentiful; and building sites were much larger than in
the cities. The frontier builders were usually less
learned and concerned with European trends and
precedents than their urban colleagues and more willing to solve problems on their own merit.

The invention of the balloon-frame construction technique, a system using small, standardized pieces of
factory-sawn wood addressed most of these problems
and suggested new forms and decorations. The style
which resulted was expressive of the "sticks" of wood
used both for the structure and as weatherboarding.
This Stick Style often bore a superficial resemblance
to medieval HALF-TIMBERED houses of which, in
several ways, it was a descendant. As take-off
points, carpenters used houses from "pattern books"
developed by designers (such as Downing). One consequently finds variations of the same basic design all
over the Midwest, elaborated or simplified according
to wealth and the skill and imagination of the
carpenter-builder.

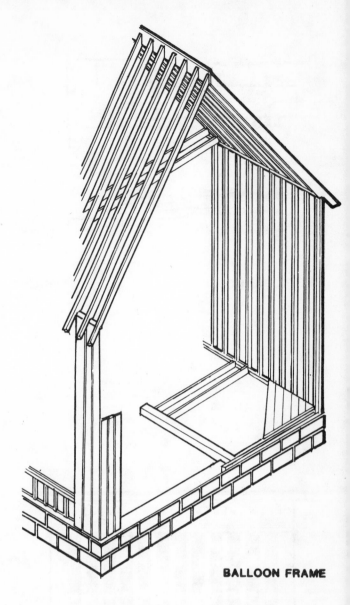

BALLOON FRAME

These variations depended upon the fact that balloon
frame construction is much more adaptable (and
cheaper) than masonry construction; its engineering is
much less critical. Consequently the plan of a house
could be modified at will; rooms made larger or smaller, windows and doors could be enlarged or grouped
together; towers and gables could easily be added. In
the extreme cases, houses became gingerbread castles
-- "carpenter gothic", as it was sometimes called.

This vernacular American architecture was eventually
taken up by trained architects like Frank Lloyd
Wright, a young architect from Chicago, and developed into the first American architecture of international stature. Influenced by his teacher Louis
Sullivan and the writings of Viollet-le-Duc, Wright
made his houses, like the Robie House (1909), seem to
belong to their sites. These Prairie Houses expressed
the flat farmland around Chicago with low, horizontal lines and shallow, spreading roofs anchored to the
ground by a central hearth and chimney. Developing
the increasingly open plans of Stick Style houses, the
rooms of the typical Prairie Style house were no
longer enclosed boxes with holes punched in some

STICK STYLE

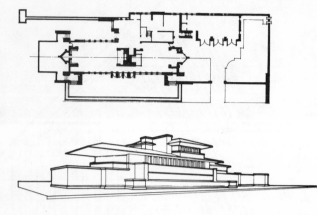

THE ROBIE HOUSE   WRIGHT

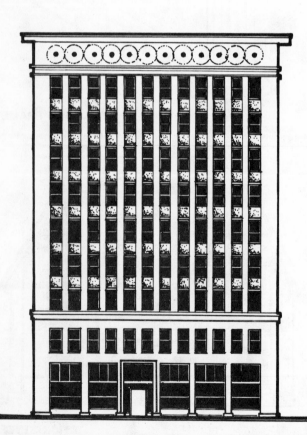

THE WAINWRIGHT BUILDING   SULLIVAN

walls for doors and others for windows. Instead, much like Horta in the Tassel House, Wright removed as many of the interior partitions as possible so that rooms flow from one into another. Often the only distinction between one major area and another was a difference in floor or ceiling height or both. Wright used strips of windows on the exterior of his buildings and banks of floor-to-ceiling glass doors that opened onto porches and patios under the hovering roofs. The exterior flows into the interior of a Wright house just as one room flows into the next.

Wright called his architecture "ORGANIC ARCHITECTURE", a concept which even he had a difficult time defining with any precision. But the "organic" way a building seems to grow out of its site; the way one space flows into the next as naturally as the trunk of a tree flows into a branch and the branch into a twig; and the concept of spaces shaped but not contained by vertical planes seemed radically new to American and European alike. Wright's ideas proved crucial to the development of architecture on the Continent; and in America, simplified and modified by contractors everywhere, it developed into the "split-level" and "ranch house" designs of today's suburbs.

Another great American innovation which altered the direction of world architecture was the multi-storied building, or skyscraper. It, too, was largely a contribution of Chicago. Two inventions were required to make the skyscraper possible: the steel skeleton ("skyscraper construction") and a safe elevator. The height of masonry buildings had been limited; for structural reasons, masonry walls become extremely thick on the ground floor, taking up much of the floor area in a really tall building. But if a cage of steel is substituted for the masonry, a building may become very tall. The steel columns of a skycraper need be very little larger at their base than they are on the top floor.

The idea of an iron-framed building seems to have been inspired by the writings of Viollet-le-Duc, but the first skyscraper was built in Chicago in 1886 (The Home Insurance Company by William LeBaron Jenney). It and many of the early skyscrapers did not look tall, however. They looked like stacks of small buildings. In 1889, beginning with the Wainwright Building in St. Louis, Louis Sullivan designed as series of tall buildings that did appear tall, that ex-

pressed the columns of steel which held them up.
They illustrated Sullivan's dictum that "Form follows
Function." Sullivan and his compatriots in Chicago
explored these new ideas in many buildings. The
"Chicago School" and Wright's Prairie Style were the
first American architecture to be respected and imitated by Europeans. They reversed the historical
directions of influence for a while.

THE INTERNATIONAL STYLE

THE FIRST GENERATION

At the time the Chicago School was flowering, the
center of AVANT-GARDE architecture in Europe was
Vienna (the Ecole des Beaux Arts in Paris was relatively conservative by comparison). In addition to a
style comparable to Art Nouveau called Secession,
Otto Wagner and his students were experimenting
with glass, steel, and aluminum in buildings which
appear strikingly modern. Another Viennese, a writer
and architect named Adolf Loos, thought architects
of his time were too preoccupied with decoration to
produce a really modern, 20th century architecture.
In 1908, after his return from a trip to Chicago, he
published an article titled Ornament and Crime in
which he equated ornamentation with decadence and
depravity and concluded that the progress of a society can be measured by the degree to which it has
eliminated decoration. This article was widely read
by young architects who saw it as a way to answer
the critics of Art Nouveau.

At about the same time, in Paris, Braque and Picasso
were revolutionizing painting. They rejected realistic,
illusionistic painting -- photography could record reality -- and, following the lead of Cezanne (a brilliant late 19th century French painter), they ana-
lyzed nature into its most characteristic shapes, reduced these to planes, and rearranged these planes
onto their canvases. The result was called Cubism.
Since Cubists paintings superimposed several different views of the same object, critics saw in them the
representation of a "4th dimension", a concept with
which contemporary scientists and mathematicians
were preoccupied. (Einstein was working out his

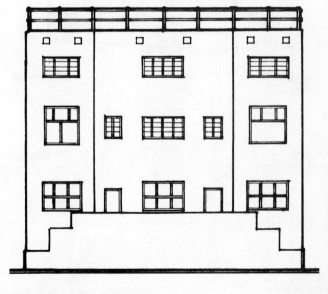

THE STEINER HOUSE   **LOOS**

AIRSHIP HANGER   **SANT'ELIA**

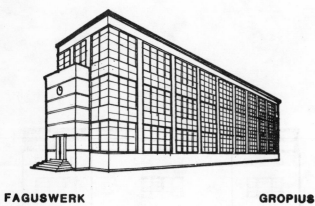

FAGUSWERK   **GROPIUS**

theories of Relativity at about the same time.) The impersonal, objective, hard-edged shapes in the Cubist paintings also appealed to contemporary critics. They looked machine-made.

The Italian Futurists were the first architects to be influenced by this revolutionary new art. Modern science and technology, the Machine Age, fascinated them. They wrote eloquently of the motor car and electric power stations; they were obsessed with speed and change. The brilliant young architect Sant'Elia (who was killed in the First World War) wrote in a manifesto of Futurist architecture that to be really modern, architecture should reject everything of the past. The architecture of the future should: 1. have no decoration (as Loos had already said); 2. make no reference to history or historical styles; 3. use only new, industrial, materials and technologies (no natural materials like wood, stone and brick) 4. use dynamic forms and shapes which derived from or resembled machines.

It was natural, then, that the factory should become an ideal prototype for Machine-age architects. The German architect Walter Gropius designed an office building (the Faguswerk) in 1911 and a school of architecture (the Bauhaus) in 1925 which were inspired by factories. In both buildings, sheer glass walls pass in front of the floors; in the Bauhaus, even the columns are behind the glass walls. The traditional idea of "carrier and carried" has been negated: the exterior wall no longer holds up the building in appearance or in reality. The variable reflectivity/transparency of the glass walls superimposed views into the buildings with reflections of the outside in a fashion which directly recalls Cubist painting. The glass box which is so characteristic of 20th century architecture has been born.

As important as the Bauhaus building itself was, the curriculum which Gropius designed for the school of architecture that occupied the building was probably even more influential. In the beginning, Gropius was influenced by the writings of Ruskin and Morris. Each student was required to learn one or more handicrafts and become expert in it before designing for that craft. Later the emphasis was shifted from handcrafted products to those which could be mass-produced by industry. Strictly speaking, no courses in architecture were taught at the school; it was assumed that the basic design principles taught in the school were sufficient training for an architect. With some modifications, many schools of architecture throughout the world still base their undergraduate curricula on the basic design course of the Bauhaus; and the furnishings designed by the faculty and students of the Bauhaus are still commonly sold in stores all over the world.

Even though Gropius eventually rejected Ruskin's and Morris' insistence on handcrafting, he retained their ideas that architecture could shape society. No one has ever fully and convincingly explained why Gropius turned to an emphasis on mass-production in his school, but the impact of the Dutch de Stijl group on Gropius and his students was one factor.

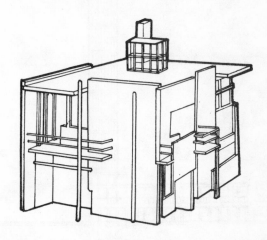

RIETVELD   **THE SCHROEDER HOUSE**

De Stijl (Dutch for "The Style") was the name of a group of artists and architects in Amsterdam which included the painter Mondrian and the architect Rietveld. They were inspired by Cubism, by Frank Lloyd Wright's buildings and new spatial concepts and by other AVANT-GARDE theories. The group wished to produce a "universal art"; they though of space as a grid extending infinitely in all directions and considered paintings and buildings to be just parts of that grid. Rietveld's Schroeder House in Utrecht was conceived as a series of vertical and horizontal planes floating in the universal grid. It is no longer tied to the idea of a specific site, nor are all of the walls permanently located. At least some of them can be slid or folded to change the interior of the house at will, making it even more "universal": it adapts to the changing needs of the inhabitant.

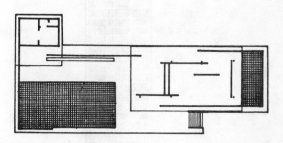

MIES   **BARCELONA PAVILION**

Mies van der Rohe, another German influenced by Wright and the de Stijl group, headed the Bauhaus after Gropius left until he, too, was forced into exile by the Nazi's (who detested modern architecture). The plan of his Barcelona Pavilion, designed for the 1929 World's Fair in Barcelona, Spain, looks like a de Stijl painting; its floating horizontal and vertical planes remind one of a Frank Lloyd Wright House. Mies manipulated plane and space in this building in such a way that any distinction between "interior" and "exterior" was entirely arbitrary. The space **implied** by the planes becomes as real and important as the solid elements. The materials, proportions and details of this building were so elegant and carefully considered, judging from photographs and descriptions -- the pavilion inexplicably disappeared after the fair ended -- that it seems more a masterpiece on a par with the Parthenon than descended from factories and Cubist/de Stijl paintings.

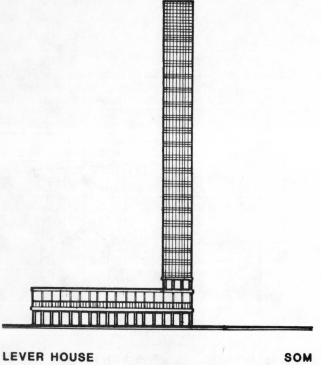

LEVER HOUSE   **SOM**

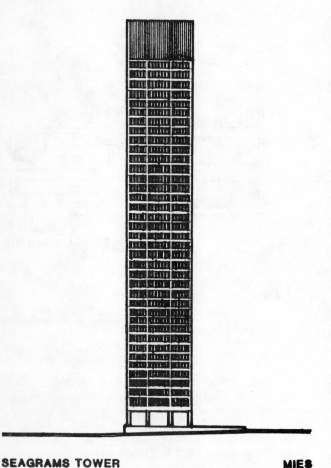

SEAGRAMS TOWER   **MIES**

Mies' skyscraper projects were among the most influential architectural designs of the 1920s. The aesthetic effect of these buildings depends on the play of light and reflection on their sheer glass facades and irregular or curvilinear plans. World War II and the Depression prevented Mies or anyone else from constructing skyscrapers based on these projects, but after the War, SOM (Skidmore, Owings, and Merrill, a Chicago architectural firm) designed Lever House in New York (1951). It was a rectangular box, rather than the sort of irregular shape Mies had projected, but the idea is the same. Mies himself, who had moved to Chicago, designed the most elegant of this type of skyscraper, the Seagrams Tower for New York City. It has a bronze and glass curtain wall which Bramante himself might have proportioned.

When Mies was made head of the school of architecture at Illinois Institute of Technology in Chicago he was commissioned to design a master plan for the university and several of its most important buildings. De Stijl influence is evident in his attempts to create a simple, universal building style. Some people have criticized this approach by saying that at IIT it's hard to know which building is the architecture building, which the chapel and which the power plant. Indeed, in following his famous dictum "Less is More," he was forced to sacrifice the naturally complicated functions of a building to this simplicity. Nonetheless, Mies designed some of the most elegant buildings in the history of man, and his glass-and-steel boxes have become the archetypical urban building of the 20th century.

There were four great Masters in the First Generation of modern architecture: Wright, Gropius, Mies and Le Corbusier. Le Corbusier (his real name was Jeanneret) was a Swiss painter/architect who lived most of his active life in Paris. He assimilated the ideas of Viollet, Horta, the Cubists, Loos and his teacher August Perret, among others. Perret had pioneered the use of reinforced concrete (concrete reinforced with steel bars that allow the concrete to resist tension). "Corbu" designed most of his structures for this new material.

If the reinforcing bars are cleverly engineered, reinforced concrete can be molded into almost any form. Perret had recreated a sort of classical, trabeated architecture with it. Le Corbusier created buildings which looked as if they had been produced by a machine. His most famous house, the Villa Savoie (1929) in the Parisian suburb of Poissy, uses sleek surfaces that appear stretched over a frame; curves which match the turning radius of the automobiles which dropped guests off at the front door; ramps like those in parking garages (in addition to stairs); exposed heating pipes and lighting fixtures and windows similar to those used in industrial buildings. "A house," wrote Le Corbusier "is a machine for living." The Villa Savoie looks like a machine for living. It is still somewhat shocking today, but once accustomed to it, most find it exciting and strangely beautiful in a classical way.

There is nothing about the Villa Savoie or the buildings of Mies van der Rohe that would suggest they belong in Paris rather than in Chicago or Hong Kong rather than in Los Angeles. Critics have often applied the term International Style to these buildings. The term refers more to their nearly universal appropriateness (and acceptance by the modern architect and his client) than to the set of common decorative or formal features that we normally mean when we use the word "style".

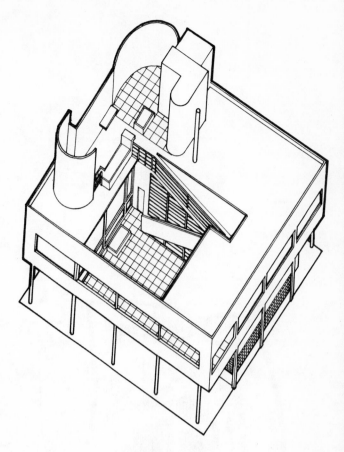

CORBU   **VILLA SAVOIE**

At its best, the International Style produced masterpieces of great refinement and technological beauty which places them alongside the great monuments of the past. At its worst, the International Style produced inhumane buildings of crushing banality because simple elegance becomes aggressively commonplace when the client is interested only about profit and his architect only in the size of his fee.

There have also been those architects and critics who criticized International Style architecture **because** it fit into one city as well as another; **because** it did not relate to local customs, materials, and climates. Frank Lloyd Wright, who had passed into a period of relative obscurity after the success of the Prairie Style, was one of them. His practice revived in the late 1930s, and he flashed into a new period of creativity. Although he condemned the International Style as soulless and inhumane, counter to his principles of "ORGANIC" architecture, he was quite evidently influenced by it. Fallingwater, a house in Pennsylvania which he designed in 1936 is a brilliant synthesis of the best qualities of the International Style and Wright's genius for wedding a building to its site through forms and materials. Its smooth concrete cantilevers recreate in manmade

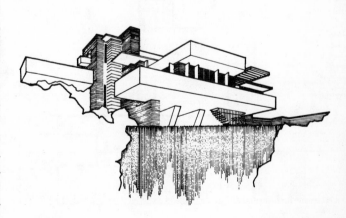

WRIGHT   **FALLINGWATER**

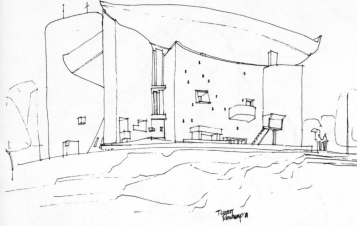

RONCHAMP

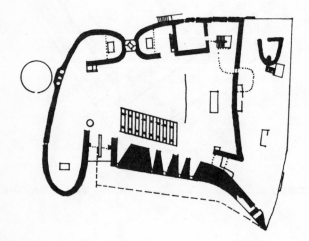

RONCHAMP   **PLAN**

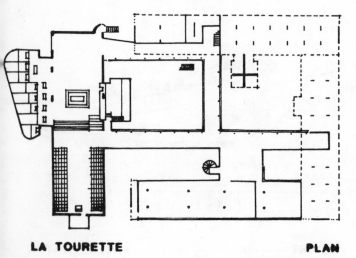

LA TOURETTE   **PLAN**

forms the rock layers of the waterfall over which the house is built.

THE SECOND GENERATION

The International Style was generally accepted only after the Second World War. The Great Depression and the War itself had brought building activity in the West to a halt, and before that, the general public and most of the architecture profession were opposed, often violently, to the International Style. Only relatively small, private structures had been built by Mies, Le Corbusier and other members of the avant-garde. The Post-war recovery period brought forward new economic conditions, a different generation of client and a changed public attitude. A steadily increasing proportion of buildings began to be built along lines that had been projected in the teens, 20s and early 30s.

Ironically, several of the leading Pre-war designers had already begun to reject their earlier projects. Some were bored with simple geometry and bare, often austere forms. Some were committed to the avant-garde principle of rejecting anything which the public accepted -- including their own projects. Le Corbusier began to speak ill of his designs of the 1920s, including the Villa Savoie, and turned to a very personal, sculptural style of architecture which turned away from the industrial, highly-machined look. His chapel of Notre Dame at Ronchamp, France, (1950-55) startled and confused his admirers. It is very irregular in plan and mass; its roof is of rough-formed concrete and its walls are of thick plaster. Nothing about it seems to refer to the machine-age ideals of Le Corbusier and the other architects of the First Generation, nor does Ronchamp seem to refer to any buildings of the past. However strange and puzzling the pilgrimage church seems at first sight, almost all who visit it, peasant and architect alike, agree that Le Corbusier has produced a building which engenders a profoundly religious feeling.

Ronchamp was succeeded by another religious building, the monastery of La Tourette near Lyon, France. It, too, shows no trace of the high technology which had originally excited the First Generation. Le Corbusier violates another of the premises of the early Modernists when he defers to historical precedent. He has brilliantly evoked the medieval monastery, but, it must be stressed, with uncompromisingly modern forms and details.

It took a while for younger architects to assimilate these new directions by Le Corbusier (who was probably the most influential of the four Masters), but his city planning ideas were emulated everywhere. He hated low, dense cities like Paris and conceived of the ideal city as a series of widely-spaced sky-scrapers, set up on freestanding columns in a land-scaped park. Published as a series of projects in the 1920s and modified over the following decades, Corbu's ideal "city in a park" was first tried out in practice just after the Second World War. The most famous of these was the Unité d'Habitation (1952) in Marseilles (only one unit of a group of skyscrapers was actually completed). He replaced the old city street with a special shopping floor half way up the building, and treated the roof as a playground and garden. With the Marseilles Unité as a model, Le Corbusier's ideas of city planning were used around the world for urban renewal and mass housing. Too often the worst aspects of Corbu's ideas were copied and the better ideas misunderstood. The isolated towers destroyed the close-knit social patterns of the neighborhoods they replaced and were unmitigated disasters when low budgets eliminated amenities like the roof terraces and landscaping around the blocks. The Pruitt-Igoe (1952-55) housing project in St. Louis proved so detested by its inhabitants that the city was forced to dynamite most of it in 1972.

Commercial success turned the once-shocking aspects of the International Style into cheap clichés. The leading younger architects (the Second Generation), bored with these banal structures, began to reject the very notion of a "universal style" of architecture, suggesting instead that each building should have its own, special identity which varied with client, site and context (the immediate physical surroundings). The International Style was appropriate for only certain types of buildings. The Finnish-American architect Eero Saarinen, for example, used a Mies-like aesthetic for the General Motors Technical Center where a machine-age image was appropriate, but he used more decorative and sculptural forms (much as Le Corbusier at Ronchamp) for others. In the terminal for Trans World Airlines at Kennedy Airport in New York, Saarinen created non-functional but soaring and expressive shapes in concrete; and in a series of dormitories at Yale University he, as Corbu had done at la Tourette, turned to the Middle Ages for inspiration.

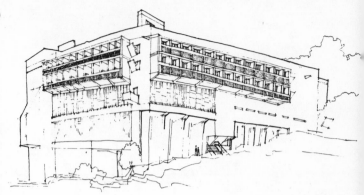

LA TOURETTE

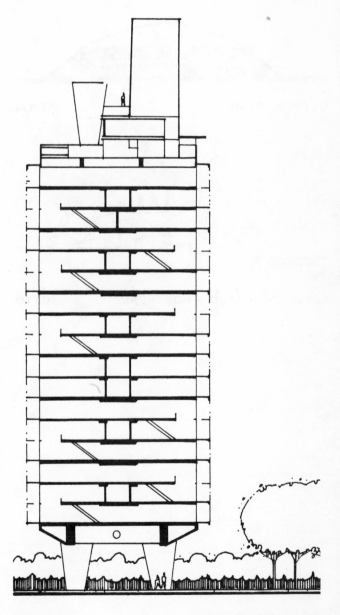

SECTION   UNITE d'HABITATION

Paul Rudolph, another leader of the Second Generation, developed sculptural towers to fit the Arts and Architecture Building at Yale into its neo-gothic context and make it stand out on a prominent corner. Widely admired for its spatial complexity when it was built, it was soon criticized for being too self-conscious and for ignoring the needs of the people who used the building. It burned in the late '60s, perhaps set on fire as a protest by the students who used it. (The fire may have been an accident, but student protestors used the it as an excuse to criticize the building, in any case.)

The more orthodox modern architects (who considered themselves "Functionalists") criticized these Second Generation architects for sacrificing function to form and for not clearly expressing the structure of the building on its exterior. This was, for the most part, a revival of the old "Rationalist" versus "Formalist" controversy.

OLYMPIC STADIA   **NERVI**

Some of the structural engineer-architects of the period such as the Italian Nervi (Rome Olympic Stadia), the German Frei Otto (the German Pavilion at the Montreal World's Fair and the Munich Olympic pavilions), the American Buckminster Fuller (the GEODESIC DOME) and the Spaniard Felix Candella (thin-shell concrete vaults) experimented with new structural systems which rendered the Functionalist (Rationalist)/Formalist controversy irrelevant. In their buildings, carrier and carried are one and the same thing. The structure is the form of the building.

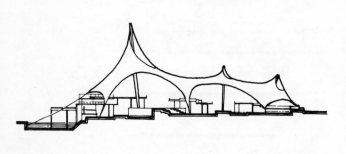

GERMAN PAVILION - MONTREAL   **OTTO**

The most avant-garde of the Second Generation also avoided the Rationalist/Formalist controversies. They took forms from a non-architectural context and turned them into buildings. The Archigram group from London used comic books, oil refineries, and even insects as sources for their buildings. They also declared that process and change should be substituted for delight in the Vitruvian triad because modern society changes so rapidly and is so mobile; parts of their buildings were designed to move or change with the changing needs of the inhabitants (the "plug-in" city). One Archigram project was for an entire city which moved wherever its inhabitants wanted to go. Most of this type of architecture, like the earlier and comparable Futurist architecture, remained on paper, but Piano and Rogers used Archigram imagery in their design for the new museum of modern art in Paris (the Centre Pompidou) which was built in 1972. The Metabolists in Japan also pursued directions parallel to the Archigram group. Although these buildings look very functional and technological, in many cases they aren't: technology is used for its sensational effects.

These are only several of the directions explored by Second Generation architects in an attempt to find a modern style to replace the International Style of the First Generation. There were many others. The unprecedented wealth in the West during this period permitted architects and engineers to experiment with an astonishing variety of forms and structural techniques. Typically, little concern was given either to the context of the buildings or to their energy consumption in the headlong search for something new and different. James Stirling of England created a number of striking buildings by combining references to Futurist architecture with Archigram-like ideas and references to 19th century buildings like the Crystal Palace. In the US, Richard Meier was one of several architects who revived the aesthetic of the early Le Corbusier. John Hejduk experimented with de Stijl forms. The only thing which ties all these Second Generation architects together is their dissatisfaction with the limitations of the First Generation. They have all reacted to one of more of the characteristics of the International Style. In hindsight, we can see references to the near and far historical past begin to creep into architecture -- in contrast to the First Generation who wished to start each project with a clean slate, free of historical memories.

Louis Kahn also reacted to First Generation forms and principles, but he was more immediately influential than most of the other Second Generation. His philosophies and buildings assimilated and synthesized so many (sometimes apparently conflicting) ideas that they served as the springboard for widely divergent points of views in others. He is the only American architect of his generation with a worldwide reputation and influence. Kahn rejected the "less is more" approach to architecture and interpreted the dictum "forms follows function" in a poetic, metaphysical way ("What does this building want to be?"); he included forms and compositional techniques that had been avoided as "messy" or "impure" in the First Generation. His buildings were rich in allusions to many periods of history, especially to those where the play of light over form and through space was as masterful as in his structures. Kahn reemphasized the

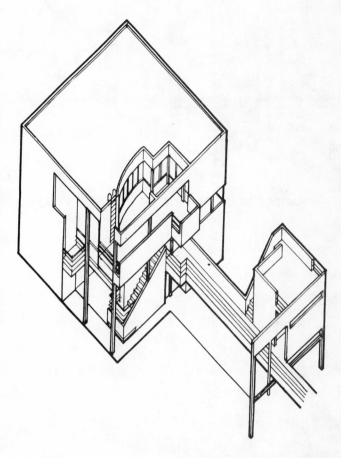

MEIER   THE HANSELMAN HOUSE

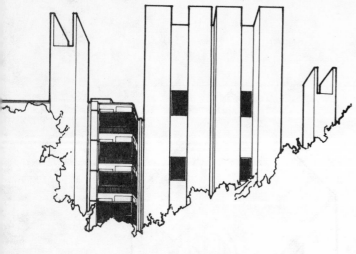

RICHARD'S MEDICAL CENTER   **KAHN**

Rationalist theory that decoration derives from the patterns left by the construction of the building.

The Richards Medical Center for the University of Pennsylvania was Kahn's first famous structure. It gave poetic feeling to the expression of the different functional areas of the plan and was one of the most imitated buildings of the mid-century. Kahn separates the laboratories (the "served" spaces) into one set of blocks and the services (stairs, air-ducts, etc.) -- the "servant" spaces -- into another set. The resulting building looks both modern and like a medieval castle.

Robert Venturi, one of Kahn's followers and the author of an immensely controversial and influential book on architecture, Complexity and Contradiction in Architecture, followed along one line of Kahn's philosophies, the willingness to include more than one type of form or compositional device in the same building (the "inclusivist" approach). He argued that "less is a bore" and that buildings should reflect the natural complexity of life; the simple forms of the First Generation were possible only because they excluded the expression of functions which would complicate plans and elevations ("exclusivist" approach).

Even more controversial among architects was his demand that they respond to what the average person builds and likes rather than try to impose sophisti-cated architectural theories and forms. "Main Street is almost all right," wrote Venturi. He meant that the neon signs, billboards and suburban houses that line most main streets in America are the real modern culture and should be the source of the architect's design vocabulary. He designed buildings along high-ways that resembled abstracted billboards. He called them "Build-ing boards."

In effect Venturi has rejected any traditional concept of beauty. His Guild House (1960-65) makes no attempt to be attractive; rather, it is intentionally made to resemble the banal, speculative apartment buildings in the neighborhood; its major piece of dec-oration is a television antenna -- not because tv antennas are beautiful but (says Venturi) because tel-evision is the most meaningful part of life for the elderly who live in the building.

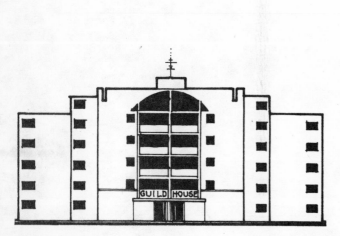

GUILD HOUSE   **VENTURI**

POST-MODERN ARCHITECTURE

A very curious thing happened as a result of the Enlightenment obsession with classification: people became aware of their place in history. Until that time, people and societies had a rather hazy notion of what had happened in the past and when it had occurred -- if they were at all concerned. "History" meant stories which pointed out some useful moral. **When** an event happened (and, in fact, **if** an event actually happened) was of little importance. For the people of the Renaissance, for example, the Roman Empire had occurred "a long time ago." Everything in between was "barbaric". None of these cultures were aware of producing art or architecture of a certain "style"; that is, it would never have occurred to Bramante that he was designing buildings in the "High Renaissance style".

The concept of style, like the classification systems of biology and zoology, was introduced in an attempt to find patterns in the phenomena of the world, to find "universal laws" that explained where we'd been, and, by extension, where we were going. As strange as it sounds to us today, such questions were of no interest to anyone before the Renaissance and of very little interest before the Enlightenment. Newton, however, found that three statements could group and explain what had seemed to be a number of unrelated physical events. Linnaeus discovered that there were not a vast number of individual plants and animals, but that they could be arranged in a few related families. In the same way, scholars grouped art and architecture chronologically according to "style": families of attitudes toward structure, decoration, compositional devices, etc. Architects were made aware of and attempted to produce buildings in a certain style: a "Romanesque" style; a "Gothic" style and -- eventually -- a "Modern" style.

Strictly speaking, "modern" means what is being done at the moment. The Eiffel Tower was "modern" in 1889. But we have come, with respect to architecture, to use the term "Modern" to refer to the architecture of the First and Second Generations as we have described it. The "Modern Style" has less of the formal coherence of the traditional historical styles (although one can certainly recognize at a glance that a Modern building is Modern rather than from some other period). The real common denominator, the basic tenet, of Modern architecture is the rejection of any specific references to the historical past. A building was not considered Modern if it used the Greek Orders; or if Gothic decorative motifs were used; or if anything which a critic could directly associate with a building of the past was used. Indeed all decorative features were avoided if possible because most buildings of the past had been decorated. The Modern architect was trying to produce something entirely new for what he saw was an entirely new age.

As we have seen, architects gradually began to accept references to history in their architecture. Le Corbusier based La Tourette on a study of Medieval monasteries. Saarinen studied the plans of Medieval towns when he was designing dormitories at Yale. This practice was criticized to varying degrees, but it was generally accepted as long as the references to the past were not explicit; as long as the architects were using the principles of historical buildings but not the specific forms or details.

It becomes difficult, however, to draw a distinctive line between using the "principle" of a gothic, pointed, arch and reviving the use of the gothic arch. Almost inevitably, architects would cross the line, and they were looked down on by the leaders of the profession for being unconverted heathens or, worse, heretics to the faith.

Nonetheless, the young leaders have begun using details from historical buildings again during the last decade -- even the Orders. To most of the architectural profession, this is still heresy. Has the basic tenet of Modern architecture been rejected? Perhaps. Those who think it has, refer to the works of these young architects (for better or worse) as "Post-Modern", the next "style" after Modern.

The Post-Modern architects are not reviving historical styles as the 19th century Eclectics (or in a sense the Renaissance architects) did, however. They are taking isolated historical details and transforming them into something "new" by changing their original function, size or scale; or parodying them: setting a keystone on top of a column, for example; or making an Ionic capital out of stainless steel. There is something Mannerist about this, something like Giulio

Romano had done with High Renaissance architecture, but in more than one respect the practice is still Modernist. The Post-Modernists are still trying to shock -- a top priority of the First Generation. In the second place, they are still, ironically, rejecting history; but they are rejecting **recent history;** they are rejecting the First Generation's rejection of history, a neat little paradox much appreciated by many of the Post-Modernists. Is there, then, such a thing as Post-Modernism? Or is Post-Modernism just another phase of the Avant-garde Modernism?

We are really too close in time to tell, too personally involved in what is going on to have any degree of objectivity. Personal feelings -- friendships with or enmities toward the individual architects color our judgements.

Phillip Johnson, for example, enraged most architects when he designed one of the first important "Post-Modern" buildings, the AT&T headquarters in New York City. He is one of the elder statesmen of the American architectural profession and was one of the leading architects of the Second Generation. In fact it was he who first used the term "International Style" in the 1930s, and he was Mies van der Rohe's collaborator on that parthenon of the Modern Movement, the Seagram's Building. That made his use of a pediment on top of the AT&T skyscraper and a motif borrowed from Brunelleschi for the entrance especially irritating. It was, for many of the more established architects, as if the Pope had suddenly declared he was an atheist.

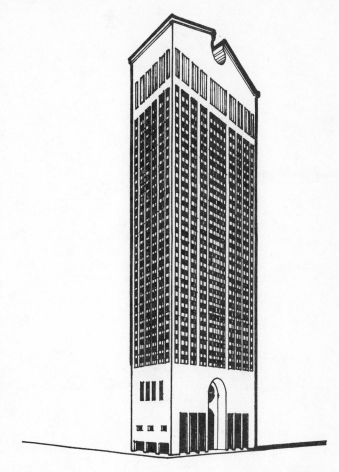

JOHNSON   **AT&T BUILDING**

Johnson has since designed a skyscraper that looks like an all-glass version of one of the towers of London's neo-gothic Houses of Parliament. Robert Venturi has used plywood silhouettes of the Doric Order on his houses, and Michael Graves (probably the most fashionable of the Post-Modern architects) has stirred great controversy with his Portland Office Building (completed in 1972). It uses super-scaled keystone motifs, details from neo-classical buildings of the 1930s and applied decoration. As many of the Post-Modernists themselves have observed, these non-traditional historical decorations are illusions no deeper than a layer of paint or an appliqué of plywood or cardboard. They may not last long enough to argue much more about.

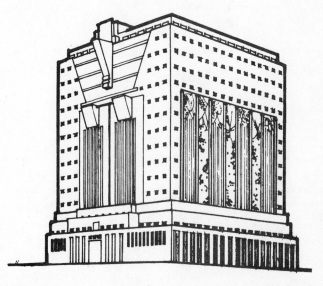

GRAVES   **PORTLAND OFFICE BUILDING**

We do not want to give the impression that Post-Modernism is the major or even the predominant new direction in architectural theory and practice. There are "high-tech" architects who try to give their buildings space age/computer age imagery (much as the First Generation used machine-age imagery) by emphasizing technical components: heating and air-conditioning ducts, elevators and escalators and highly machined, polished, industrially produced surfaces. There are architects (especially in Europe) who believe that Marxism should be the dominant political philosophy and should determine architectural form. There are "contextualists" who think that all these other concerns are less important than designing buildings which defer in character and materials to those already in existence around it.

It is not clear what direction will emerge as the predominant style in this period of architectural pluralism. But it was undoubtedly not clear in the early 15th century that the sort of direction Brunelleschi was taking would become the predominant architectural style of the next century or so, and it is only the clear vision of hindsight that allows us to see certain buildings as leading up to the Baroque style which Bernini popularized.

We have chosen to discuss Post-Modernism, as we have chosen examples elsewhere in this brief introduction to architecture, because it allows us to make certain points more easily than other examples might. Besides showing that architects are re-examining our historical past in an attempt to create an ever more humane built environment, Post-Modernism points up the increasingly important role the media have played in shaping architectural theory ever since the first architectural magazines were introduced in the 19th century. The media are largely responsible for the fame and influence of Post-Modernism because they have selected it as their darling from among the many exciting directions being pursued in this volatile period. The active role of the media is both good and bad. Magazines and television can make innovations and brilliant designs known immediately and widely, but they can also give unwarranted publicity to people who have special access to the publishers or who design sensational buildings that "make good press."

Indeed the mainstream of architecture, the vast majority of buildings, is not very well represented in the press -- or in this book for that matter -- simply because the unusual is the most newsworthy. Main-stream architecture is what we really deal with in our everyday life, however, and is for many valid reasons neither avant-garde nor particularly innova-tive. Some of the mainstream is very conservative in fact. Banks and houses and churches are being built every day in an "Early American" style, for example, and pizza parlors are being built to look like pueblos.

First and Second Generation architecture is still the model for the bulk of what architects design, how-ever, despite Post-Modernism and other avant-garde trends, though it is the rare architectural firm whose buildings do not in some degree show the influence of the avant-garde. This is how architectural style changes: some innovations of avant-garde buildings are assimilated into the mainstream bit by bit. Over a period of time the mainstream is completely re-newed in the incessant search by architects to reflect the values of a society, to communicate and reinforce them to the society itself and to leave an artistic legacy for the future.

We have chosen to illuminate our survey with exam-ples of the pioneering works, the architectural leaven, followed by a characteristic building from the mainstream that was eventually influenced. It should be pointed out that pioneering works often have the flaws as well as the excitement of the new and un-tried. Imhotep's Step Pyramid was not as refined as the Great Pyramid; Louis Kahn's Richards Medical Center is not nearly as good a building as, for exam-ple, his later Salk Institute. In both cases, the inno-vations the architects made had to be tested and re-fined, but in both cases the pioneering works were brilliant despite their shortcomings and so wildly in-fluential that one need make no apologies for their "warts".

One last comment is appropriate regarding "pioneer-ing" or avant-garde works. We need them, but we don't need too many of them. Architectural chaos would result, and architects would never have enough time to sort out the unsuccessful innovations and re-fine the promising ones.

It is a characteristic of the pioneer or avant-gardist to superimpose some pre-conceived philosophical con-cepts on his clients. The Renaissance architect, for example, forced the centralized plan on an unwilling clergy. The Post-Modernists are adding their gratui-tous historical references to buildings for their own

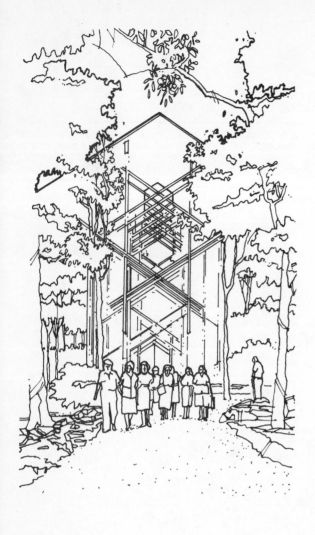

THORNCROWN CHAPEL   **JONES**

reasons. Most architects must -- and do -- try to balance their own theories and predilections with the needs of the clients, and these two with what is most appropriate for the neighborhood, the town, and society at large. When the client and the architect understand these interlocking levels of responsibility, buildings are created which enrich the lives of everyone who comes into contact with them. Most of these good buildings go unrecognized in national magazines, newspapers or on television simply because they do not call attention to themselves by being "different" or they exist in a region outside the normal scrutiny of the media. Occasionally word of mouth or an outside visitor will bring an outstanding "regional" building to the attention of others, and it emerges as a widely known and beloved masterpiece.

Such has recently happened to the Thorncrown Chapel by E. Fay Jones. It is a particularly heartening piece of architecture with which to finish our book, for Thorncrown Chapel has not become world-famous because it was a pioneering work or because it was avant-garde or sensational. Its location, near Eureka Springs, Arkansas, is not usually considered one of the cultural centers of the world; its architect was not widely known beyond his region. It has become famous simply because it is extraordinarily fine architecture; created by a fine and caring person and his fine and caring client. Thorncrown Chapel shows that good architecture is within the reach of all of us, anywhere. As Le Corbusier wrote, very eloquently, in the 20s:

> You employ stone, wood and concrete, and with these materials you build houses and palaces. That is construction. Ingenuity is at work.
>
> My house is practical. I thank you, as I might thank Railway engineers or the Telephone service.
>
> But suddenly you touch my heart, you do me good, I am happy and I say: "This is beautiful." That is Architecture. Art enters in.
>
> from Towards Architecture

FIRMITAS UTILITAS VENUSTAS

•

FIRMNESS COMMODITY DELIGHT

GLOSSARY

We have tried to explain most unfamiliar terms and
words within the body of the text. In some cases,
however, an explanation would have digressed to far
from the narrative or would have referred to material not yet covered. We have marked out such words
with capital letters and discuss them below.

AQUEDUCT A channel or pipe for carrying water.
Aqueducts are usually almost invisible utilitarian
structures given little attention by architects. But
they were made exceptionally attractive by the ancient Romans and became one of the symbols of this
society which put so much importance on structures
of civic utility. They Romans would, literally, go to
any lengths to bring the best water in the region into
their cities for bathing and drinking. Where possible
aqueducts would be buried or laid on the surface of
the ground; but where they had to cross rivers or
gorges, and where they entered cities, elaborate
arched structures, usually of striking beauty would be
built.

AVANT-GARDE Although the term is loosely applied
to anyone introducing new ideas ("Michelangelo was
avant-garde") the term is accurately used to describe
ideas and practices which began to be introduced in
the middle of the 19th century. The avant-garde began as a reaction to established art, to establishment
in general. Thus a prime intention of the avant-garde
is to do something which shocks society at large.
This implies the rejection of anything traditional and
historical. Ironically, a true avant-gardist must ne-
cessarily reject his own works, since as soon as they
are finished they become history. Because the intention of the avant-garde is to shock and offend society, they have found themselves in a dilemma: the
society they attempt to antagonize is also the society which patronizes their art; that is, they are committed to alienating the very people upon whom they
depend for their livelihood. A second dilemma is
posed by need to escalate what is needed to shock;
shock value wears off quickly, and so many things
have been attempted that it is difficult for the
avant-garde to find anything left which is shocking.

as we have described in the last section of the book, virtually the only shocking thing left for the avant-garde has been to create traditional things with historic references. Unfortunately for the avant-garde, these "traditional" objects do not shock the public. They only shock the avant-garde.

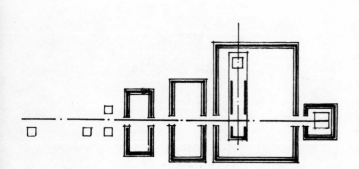

AXIS (plural AXES) An imaginary line of reference to which the constituent units of a building or a COMPLEX of buildings are related. Most commonly the term is used to describe a situation in which these units -- rooms, openings, piazzas, etc. -- are arranged symmetrically around the axis or strung along it like beads on a necklace. In complicated plans (such as Roman baths or the gardens at Versailles) minor axes are often introduced at right angles to the main axis (cross-axes) to organize subsidiary components of the plan.

BARREL VAULT see VAULT.

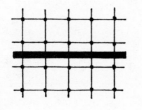

BAY The principal divisions of a building, usually marked off by columns, pilasters, buttresses and the like. For example, a Gothic church is marked off into bays by the columns. Or in a stable, each stall would be one bay (and could even house a bay).

CLASSIC, CLASSICAL, and CLASSICISM In history and criticism, these terms are given specific connotations. CLASSIC is used to describe an outstanding example of a particular genre. ("Chartres is a classic gothic cathedral.") CLASSICAL refers to the art and literature of ancient Greece and Rome. CLASSICISM is a revival of the principles of Greek and Roman art. Carolingian, Renaissance and late 18th-early 19th century architecture were all examples of classicism. The latter period is often called NEO-CLASSICISM since it was a revival of Renaissance classicism.

COMPLEX In architecture, a complex is a group of buildings which are related through form or planning to form a single entity.

CONCRETE A mixture of specific proportions of cement (calcined limestone and clay), sand or some other fine aggregate (rock fragments), coarse aggregate (gravel, small rocks or pieces of brick, etc.) and water. This viscous liquid gradually solidifies into a rock-like substance. It has been used since Roman times. If cement is mixed only with sand, quicklime and water it is called MORTAR. Mortar is used to bond units of masonry (see MASONRY) together or as a plaster. Like stone, concrete and mortar are strong in resisting compressive forces but weak in resisting tensile forces. The 19th century corrected this shortcoming by placing iron or steel bars and wires in the concrete wherever tensile forces were present. The result is REINFORCED CONCRETE, a "composite material" which has its own special structural qualities. Reinforced concrete may be formed into almost any shape, but a skilled engineer is required to calculate the size and location of the reinforcing.

CROSS A figure formed by the intersection of two or more straight lines. Crosses are among the oldest decorative signs and symbols. The cross has special significance for Christians and has often been used for the plans of Christian churches. If one arm of the Christian cross is longer than the others, it is called a LATIN CROSS (characteristic of Romanesque, Gothic, and many Renaissance Churches). If all four arms are the same length, it is called a GREEK CROSS (characteristic of Byzantine and some Renaissance architecture). If the longer arm of a cross stops at the intersection with the two shorter arms, it is called a TAU CROSS (characteristic of Early Christian architecture).

DOME A dome may be thought of as an arch rotated about a central axis to form a vault (see VAULT). The shape of the arch which forms the cross-section through the vault determines its shape: hemispherical, pointed, onion-shaped, etc. Domes are often set on cylindrical walls called DRUMS. The small decorative construction which may surmount a dome is called a LANTERN. For domes which rise above a square plan, devices must be used to make a transition from the square to the circular base of the dome. SQUINCHES are concentric, corbelled, arches which span across the corners of the square and make a polygonal form that approximates a circle. A more elegant device is the PENDENTIVE, a spherical triangle whose point rests on a corner of the square and whose base curves to touch the bases of pendentives rising from the other corners to form a circular base for the dome.

DRUM see DOME.

GEODESIC DOME A domical structure invented by Buckminster fuller which uses small members of identical dimensions to create a frame. The geometry with which these pieces is assembled is crucial to the

squinch

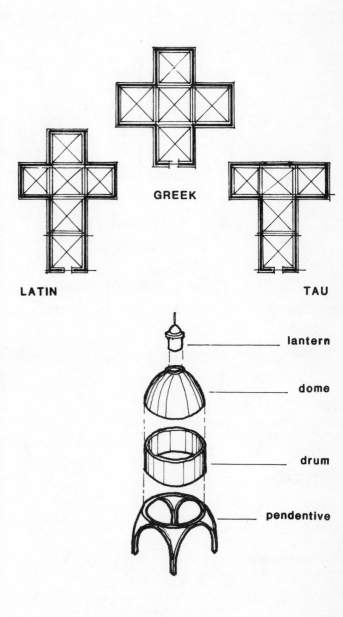

GREEK

LATIN   TAU

lantern

dome

drum

pendentive

stability of the dome and was based on studies of how a matrix can be applied to measure the surface of the earth.

GREEK CROSS see CROSS.

HALF-TIMBERING Until balloon framing was developed in the 19th century, wooden buildings were constructed of widely-spaced, heavy timbers to form an open frame. The spaces between the timbers were filled with smaller pieces of wood and nogging (plaster or brickwork). Left exposed, the wooden structure forms attractive and decorative patterns. It is sometimes plastered over or covered with horizontal boards.

LANTERN see DOME.

LATIN CROSS see CROSS.

MASONRY Anything built of brick, stone, tile or blocks (of concrete, for example).

MODULE is used in two senses in this book. 1. The basic unit of measurement for the Classical Orders (the radius of the column shaft). The dimensions of every other component of the Order are based on multiples or subdivisions of the module. 2. Any unit which is multiplied throughout a building. In Brunelleschi's Santo Spirito, for example, the crossing bay is the module. The nave is several modules in length and two modules high, the transepts are one module deep, the bays of the side aisles are quarter modules and so on. In MODULAR CONSTRUCTION, a basic unit (like a brick) is used to build the structure. The module may, of course, be larger in industrialized buildings (a standard wall panel, for example).

MOTIF A theme or dominant symbol or feature. The cross is a Christian motif.

ORGANIC ARCHITECTURE A term invented by Frank Lloyd Wright to describe his architectural philosophy. He uses it as an architectural metaphor for the principles and formal relationships he derived from nature. Since both "organic" and "nature" have many shades of meaning, the term organic architecture can mean a wide variety of things. Basically, though, Wright meant that all parts of a building should be related to each other formally and structurally as coherently as the parts of any organism in nature are informed by the same structural and formal principle. He also wished to imply that building materials should be used according to their inherent properties, just as "Nature" uses bone, cellulose and other materials in an efficient way. He did not mean, however, that buildings should **look** like natural organisms.

PENDENTIVE see DOME.

PERSPECTIVE The art and science of giving the illusion of depth and volume on a surface. There are several kinds of perspective, but when unmodified the term usually refers to linear perspective. True dimensions are projected on a surface as if seen from a particular point (the station point). Lines which are perpendicular to the plane of the viewer's body (orthogonals) appear to converge at a point (the vanishing point) in the simplest kind of perspective. You can understand the principle of perspective if you imagine looking down a railroad track: the rails seem to meet at a point on the horizon.

PHARAOH Because a spoken word had magical powers for them, the ancient Egyptians avoided saying the word "king" aloud by using the term "Pharaoh" ("Great House") to refer to their monarch (much as Americans refer to the President as "the White House").

PILASTER When the vertical element of the trabeated system is rectangular in plan, it is called a PIER (if it is small and round, it is called a POST; medium-sized and round it is a COLUMN; massive it is called a PILLAR). A shallow pier built against a wall is called a PILASTER. It looks like a strip applied to the wall, is usually decorative and may be treated like one of the Orders.

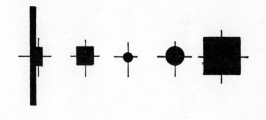

PODIUM A rectangular block on which something is set. The colonnade of a Roman temple is set up on a podium rather than the three steps of a Greek temple.

PYLON The towers, rectangular in plan but trapezoidal in silhouette, which flanked the entrance to an Egyptian temple. Hence any isolated tower structure such as the towers which hold up the cables of a suspension bridge.

PYRAMID A pyramid is a structure built on a square base with triangular sides that meet at a point. It is a Greek word meaning "wheat cake". When the

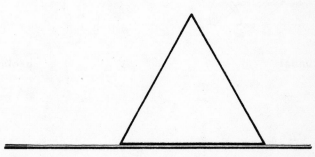

ancient Greek tourists saw the pyramids from a distance, they were reminded of the shape they baked bread.

RAFTERS The sloping "beams" in a roof structure.

REINFORCED CONCRETE see CONCRETE.

RELIEF Sculptured figures that project from a flat background (as opposed to freestanding sculpture). If the sculpture projects very little from its background, it is called LOW RELIEF (BAS RELIEF). If it projects significantly, it is called HIGH RELIEF.

RUBBLE Rough stone of irregular shape (as contrasted with cut or "dressed" stone) used in masonry construction. COURSED RUBBLE MASONRY is rubble laid in horizontal layers.

SPHINX A mythical animal with the body of a lion and the head of a man or woman. Common to both Greek and Egyptian mythology. THE SPHINX is a sculpture with the head of the Pharaoh Khephren. It is located near his valley temple and is often considered testimonial to the creative instincts of man since it appears to have been an outcropping left from the quarrying of stone for Khephren's pyramid. The idea of the sphinx seems to have appealed to the ancient Egyptians who lined great avenues in front of their temples with sphinxes.

SQUINCH see DOME.

TERRACOTTA A glazed, baked clay used in buildings for surfacing walls and, since it can be molded into almost any shape, for decorations. It was widely used in Mesopotamia and by the Etruscans. It was also used in many of the skyscrapers of the late 19th, early 20th, centuries (for example those of Louis Sullivan).

VAULT A roof or ceiling structure which has the cross section of an arch. If a vault is continuous, unbroken, and longitudinal it is called a BARREL (OR TUNNEL) VAULT. A GROIN VAULT is created when a barrel vault is intersected by barrel vaults of the same size and shape.

tunnel   groin

BIBLIOGRAPHY

Of the hundreds of excellent books available to the interested reader who wishes to know more, we would like to point out several of general interest and special merit.

general texts relating architecture to the other arts

Gardner, Helen (revised by de la Croix, Horst and Tansey, Richard G.), Art Through the Ages, New York: Harcourt, Brace & World, Inc., 1970.

Janson, H. W., History of Art, New York: Harry N. Abrams, Inc., 1962 and later revisions.

general books on architecture and its history

Ching, Francis D. K., Architecture: Form, Space & Order, New York: Van Nostrand Reinhold Company, 1979. Ching's book is particularly interesting because it groups buildings through formal similarities rather than by historical style or period.

Fleming, John; Honour, Hugh; and Pevsner, Nikolaus; The Penguin Dictionary of Architecture, Harmondsworth: Penguin Books Ltd., 1980. A paperback which explains most of the terms used by architects and architectural historians. The hardbound edition (Woodstock, N. Y.: The Overlook Press, 1976) is much more extensive and profusely illustrated.

Fletcher, Sir Bannister (revised by Palmes, J. C.), A History of Architecture, New York: Charles Scribner's Sons, 1975. THE encyclopedia of architecture. It contains plans, sections and drawings of most of the important historical buildings. The illustrations and factual data are more important than the text.

Kostoff, Spiro (editor), The Architect: Chapters in the History of the Profession, New York: Oxford University Press, 1977. A history of architects rather than a history of architecture.

Nuttgens, Patrick, The Pocket Guide to Architecture,
    New York: Simon and Schuster, 1980. An
    extremely useful survey of architecture,
    especially for the traveller, since it is
    literally pocket-sized and relatively complete.

Pevsner, Nikolaus, An Outline of European
    Architecture, Harmondsworth: Penguin Books
    Ltd, revised 1974. The standard general
    history of architecture in the West.

Rasmussen, Steen Eiler (translated from the Danish
    by Wendt, Eve), Experiencing Architecture,
    Cambridge: M. I. T. Press, c. 1962. A charming
    book on how to appreciate architecture -- and
    why

more specialized studies

Because the most histories of architecture usually
treat the modern period in less detail than other historical periods, the following two books are recom-
mended even to the general reader:

Benevolo, Leonard, History of Modern Architecture
    (two volumes), Cambridge, Mass.: the M. I. T.
    Press, 1977.

Frampton, Kenneth, Modern Architecture: A Critical
    History, London: Thames and Hudson, 1980.

Each period of history is treated in depth in the
excellent Pelican History of Art series published by
Penguin Books.

INDEX

index

124

index

NOTES

NOTES

NOTES

NOTES